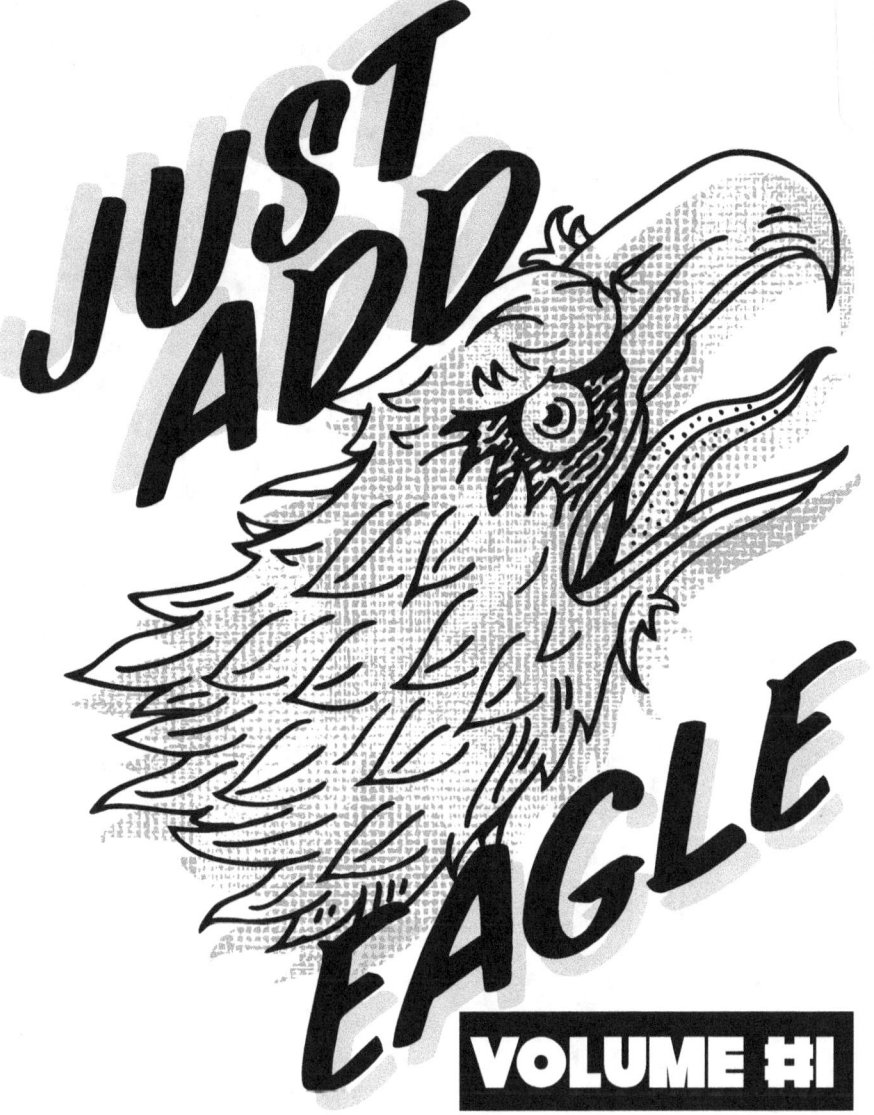

JUST ADD EAGLE

VOLUME #1

ART + LETTERING 'ZINE

**ALL ART (C) 2020
CJ HUGHES
WWW.CJHUGHESLETTERING.COM
615-482-2839**

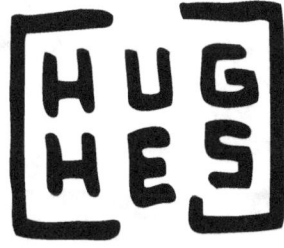

@CJHUGHESLETTERING

ABCDEF
GHIJKLM
NOPQRST
UVWXYZ
12345678
90

CREATED WITH A CRAYOLA BROAD TIP MARKER.

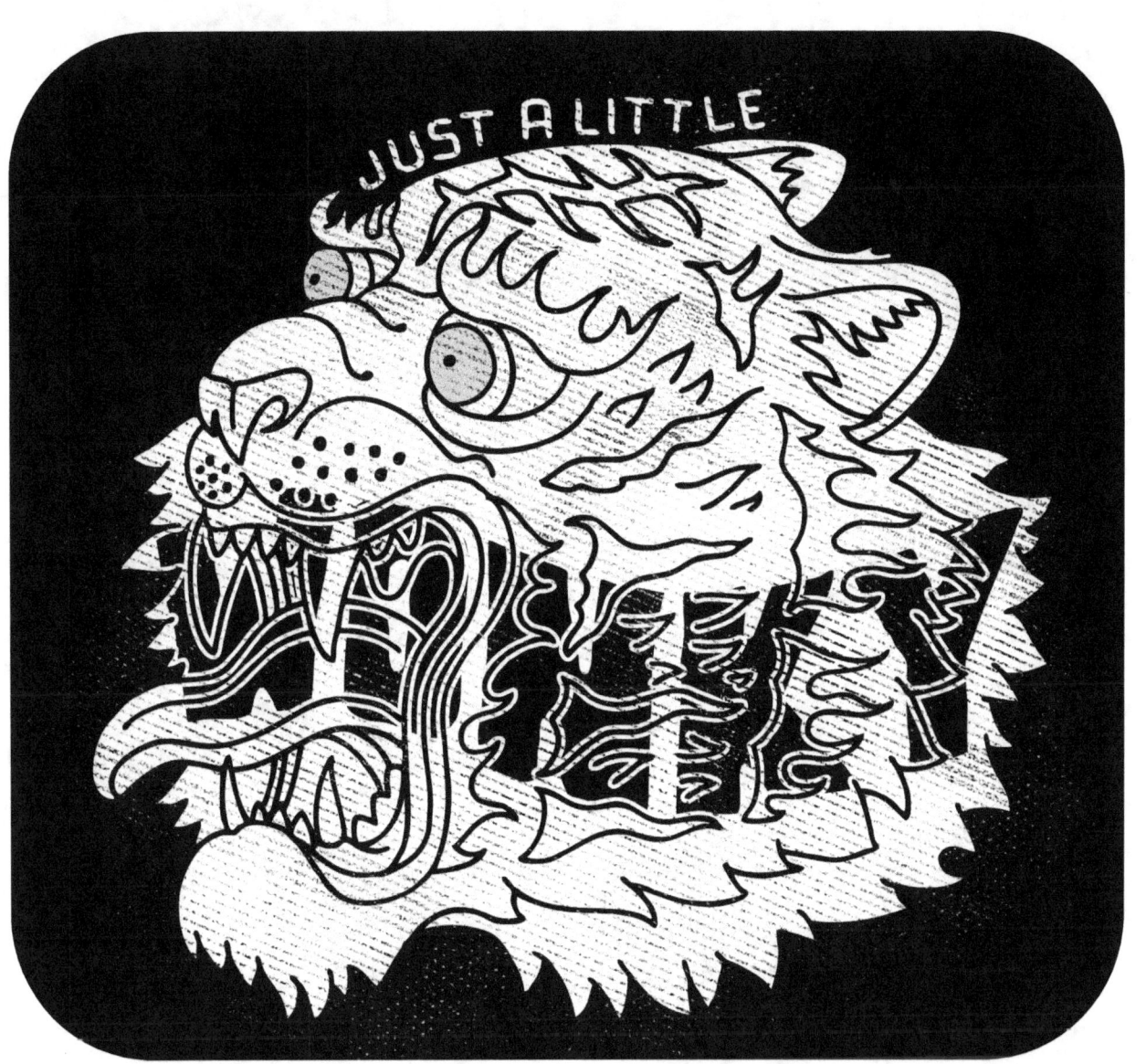

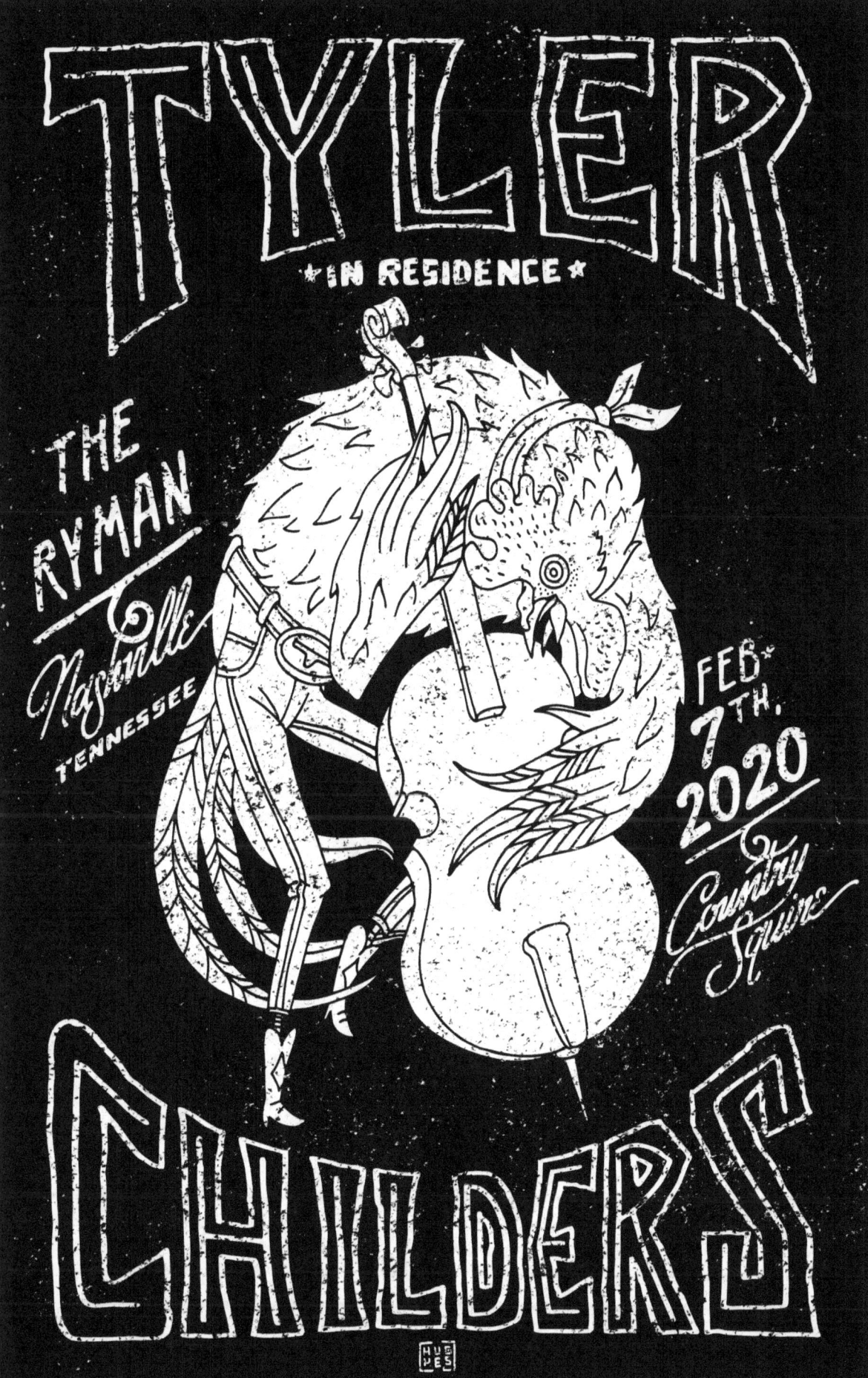

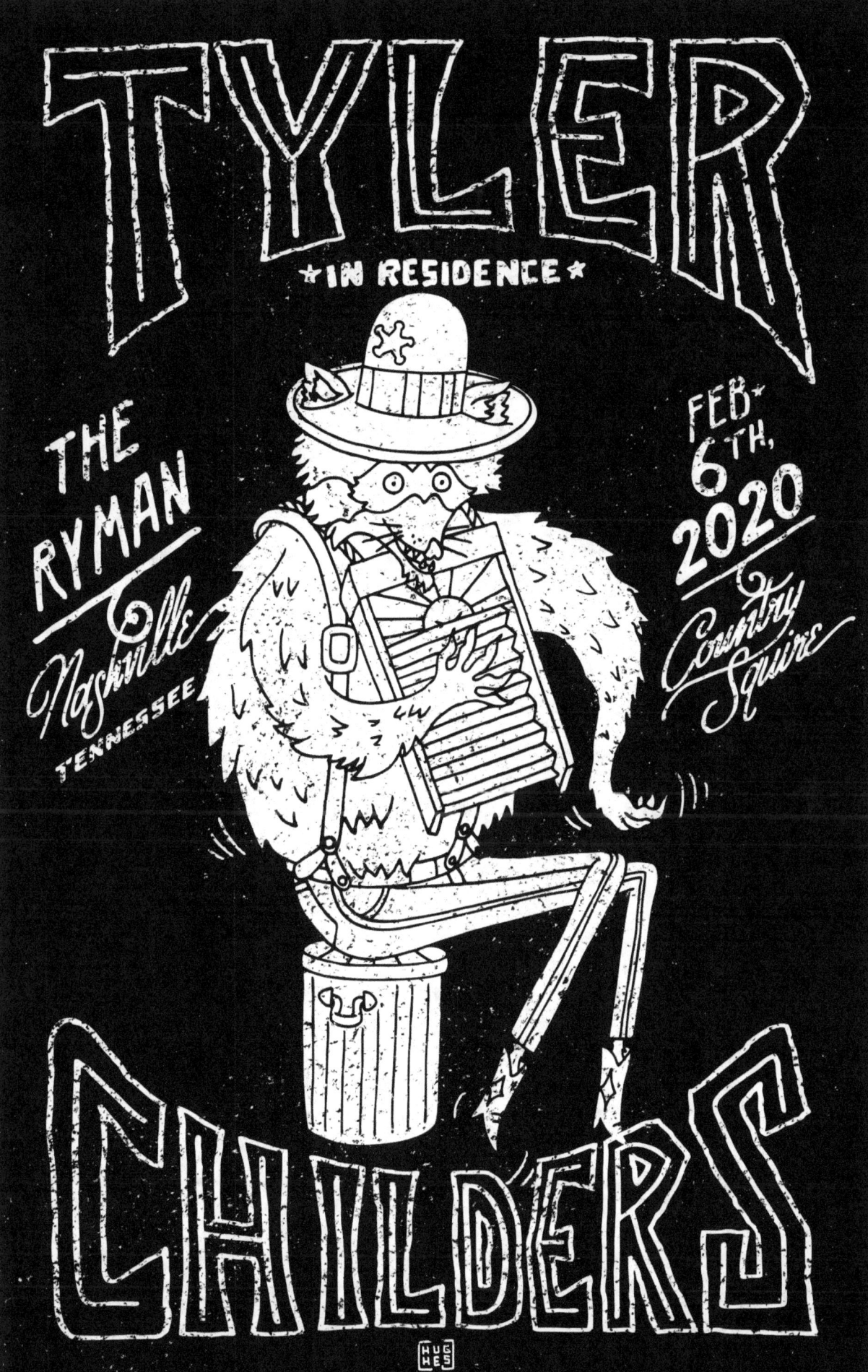

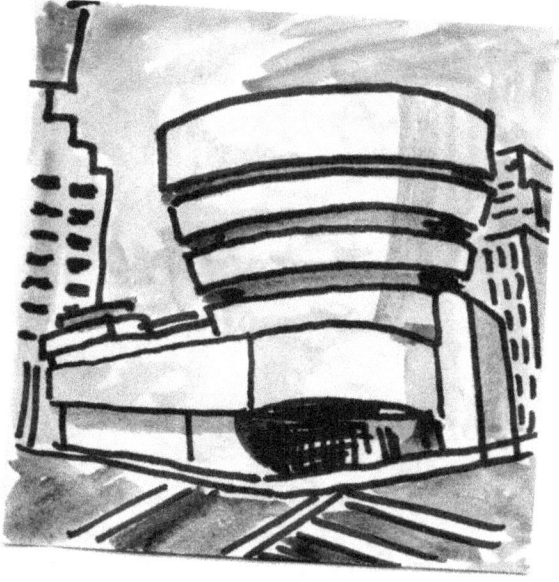
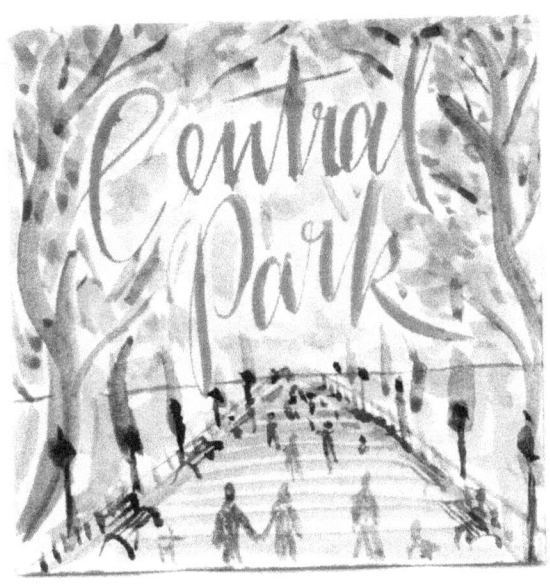
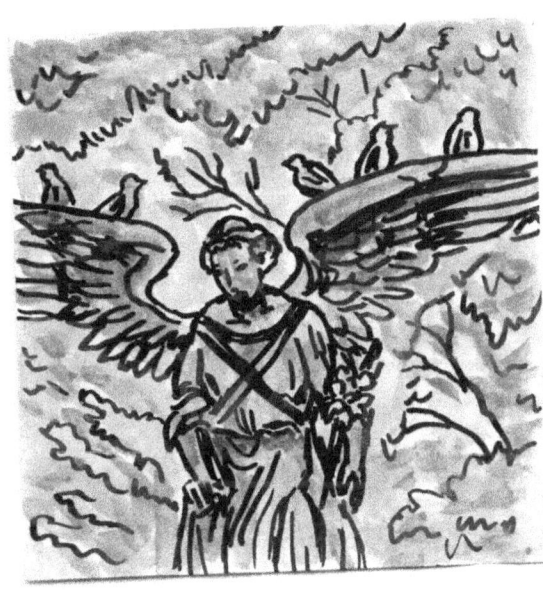
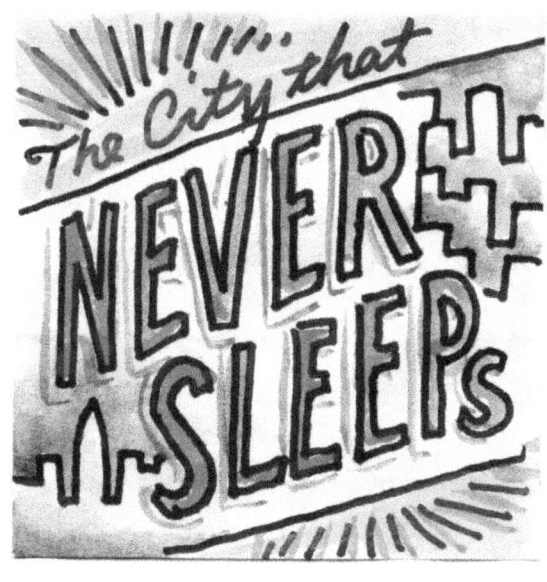
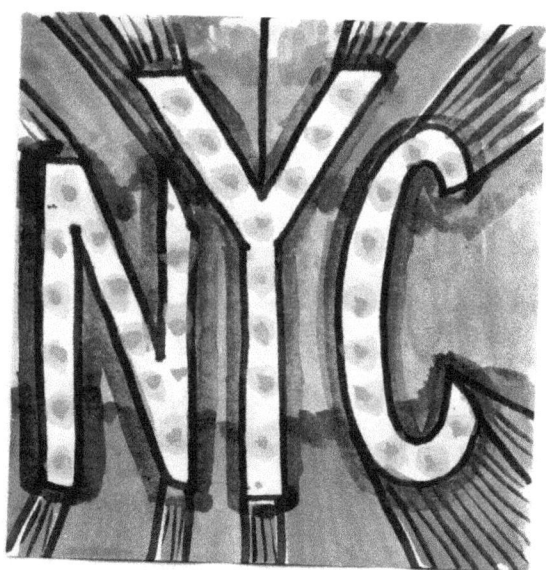

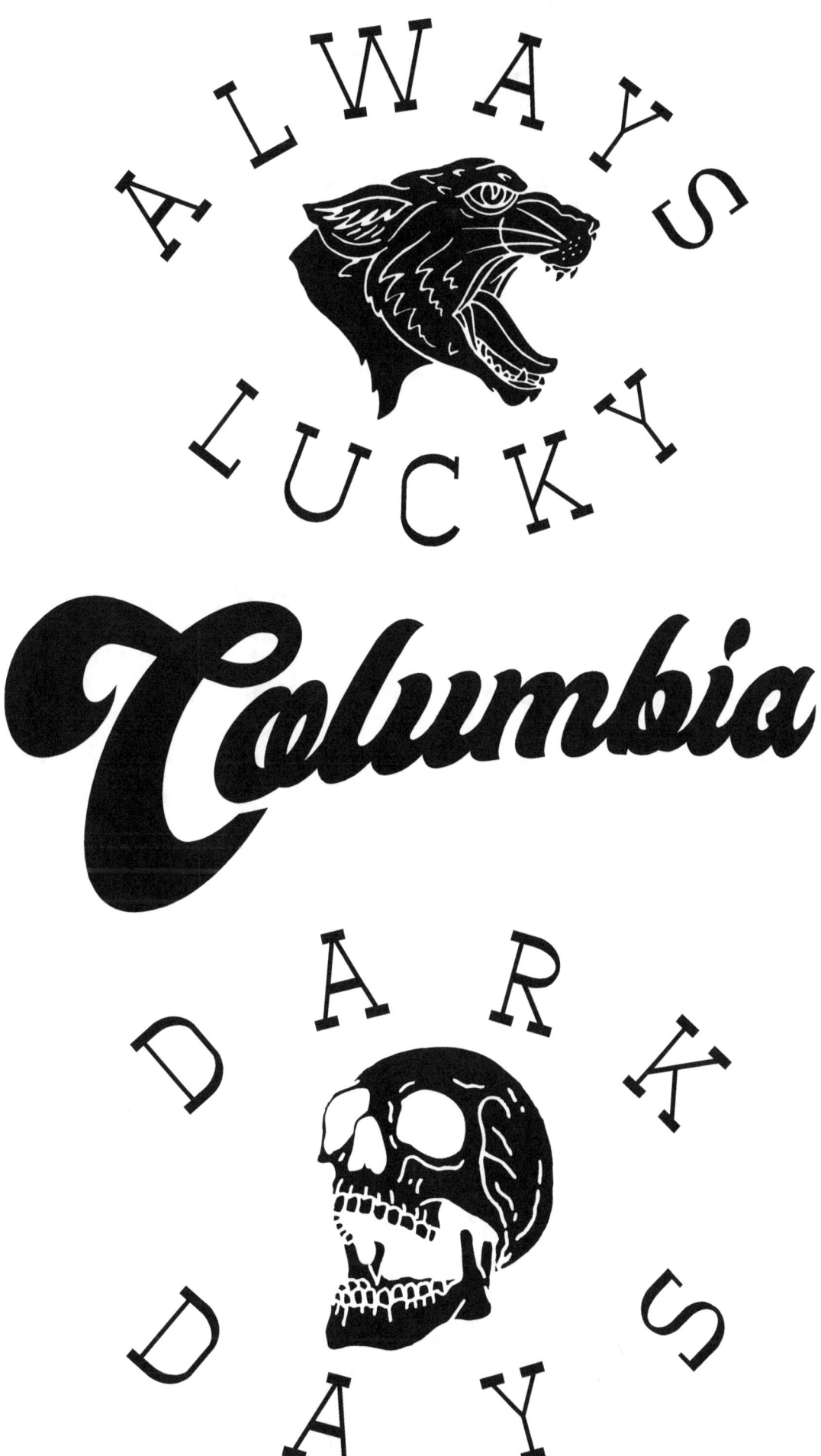

ABCDE
FGHIJK
LMNOPQ
RSTUVW
XYZ

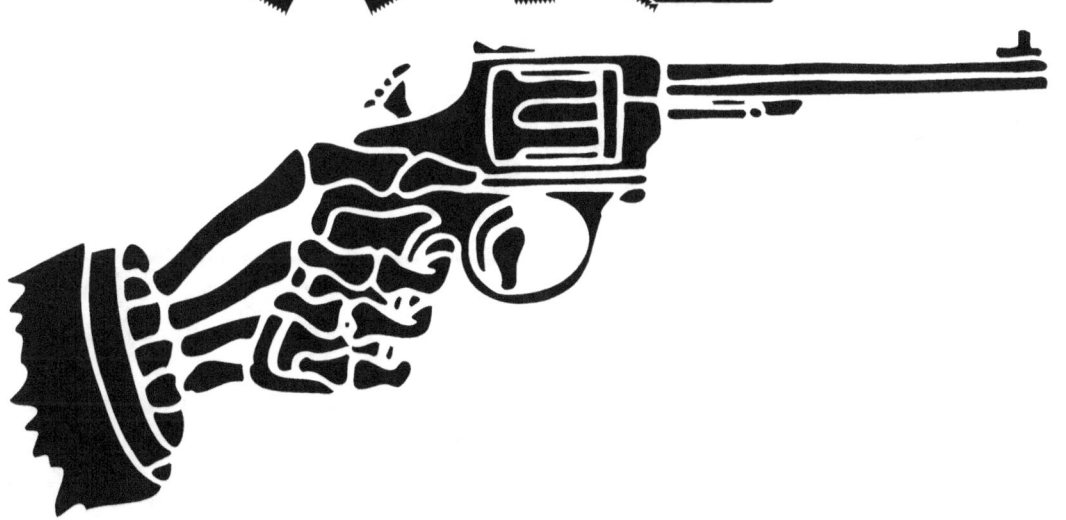

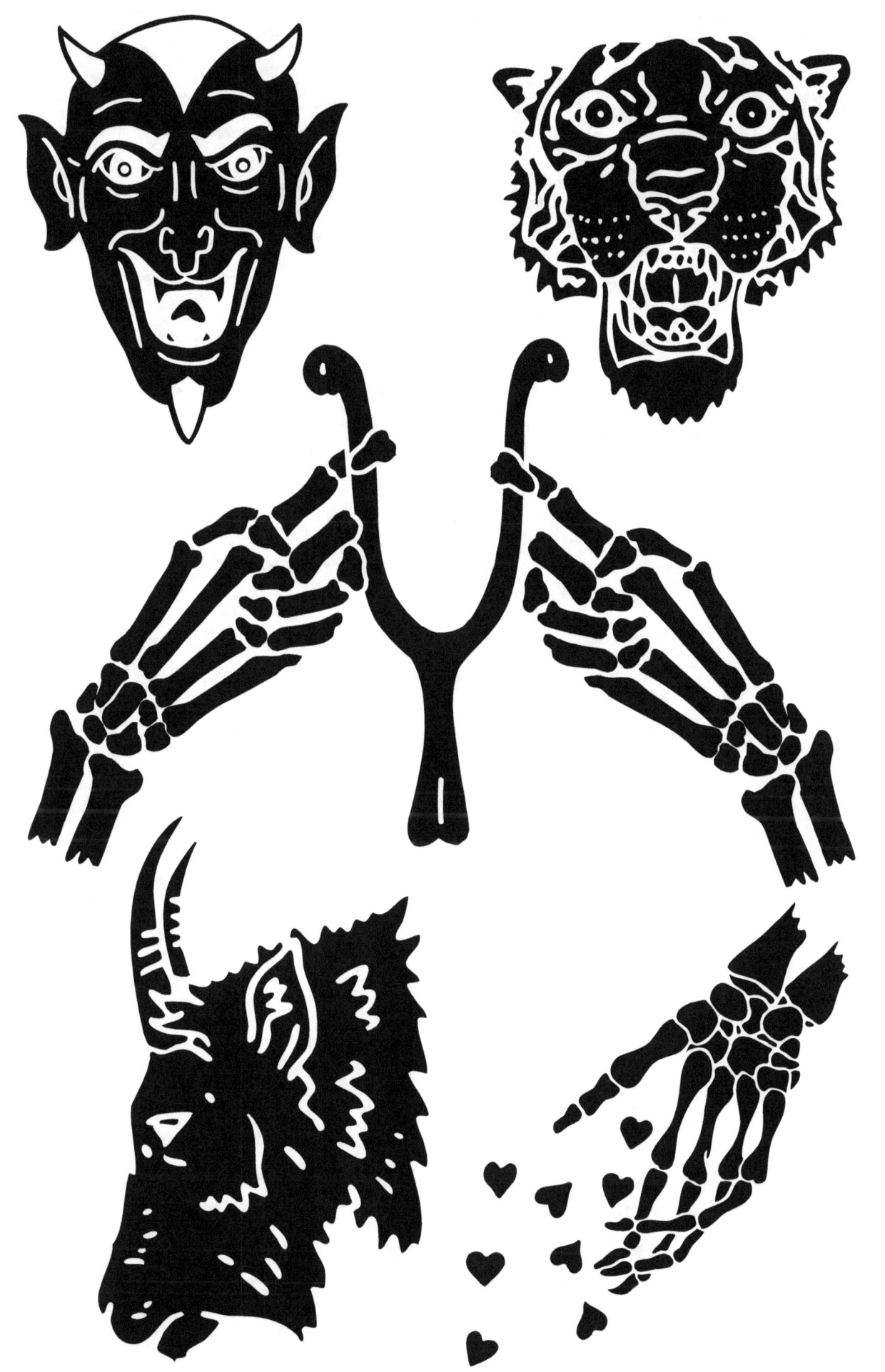

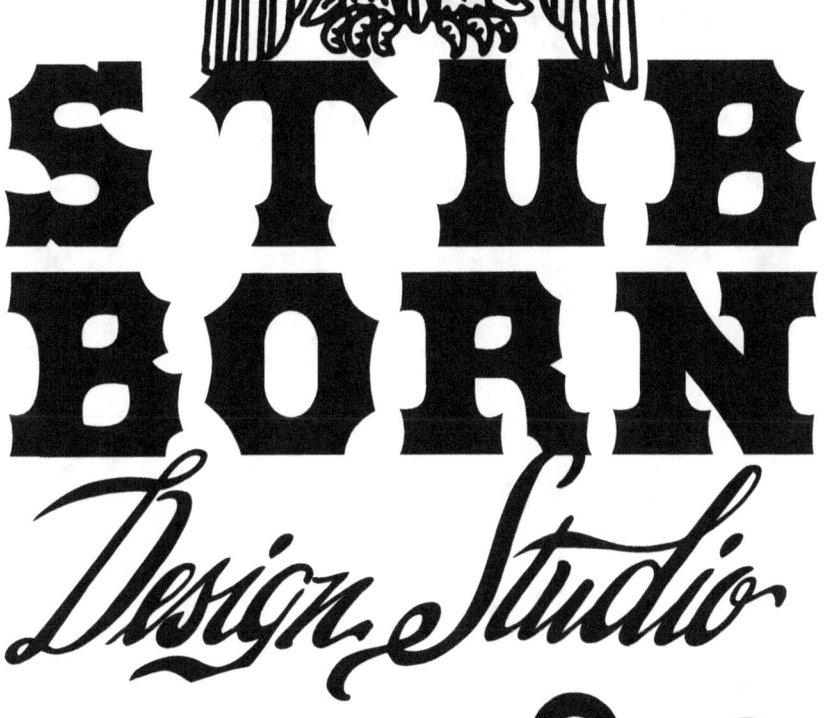
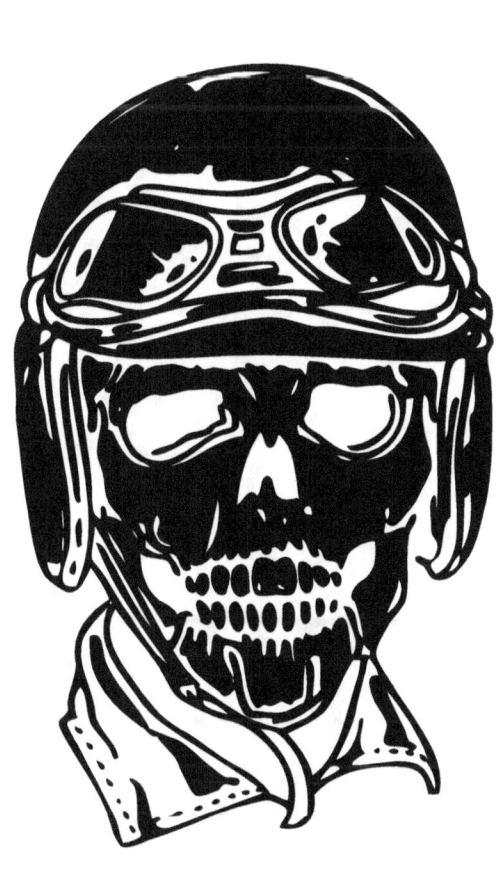
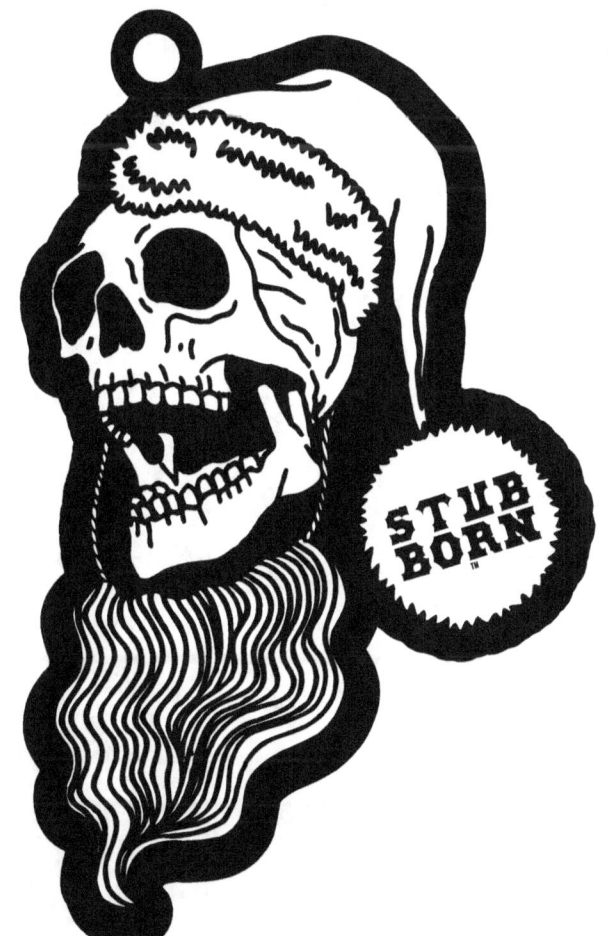

Vintage Beer

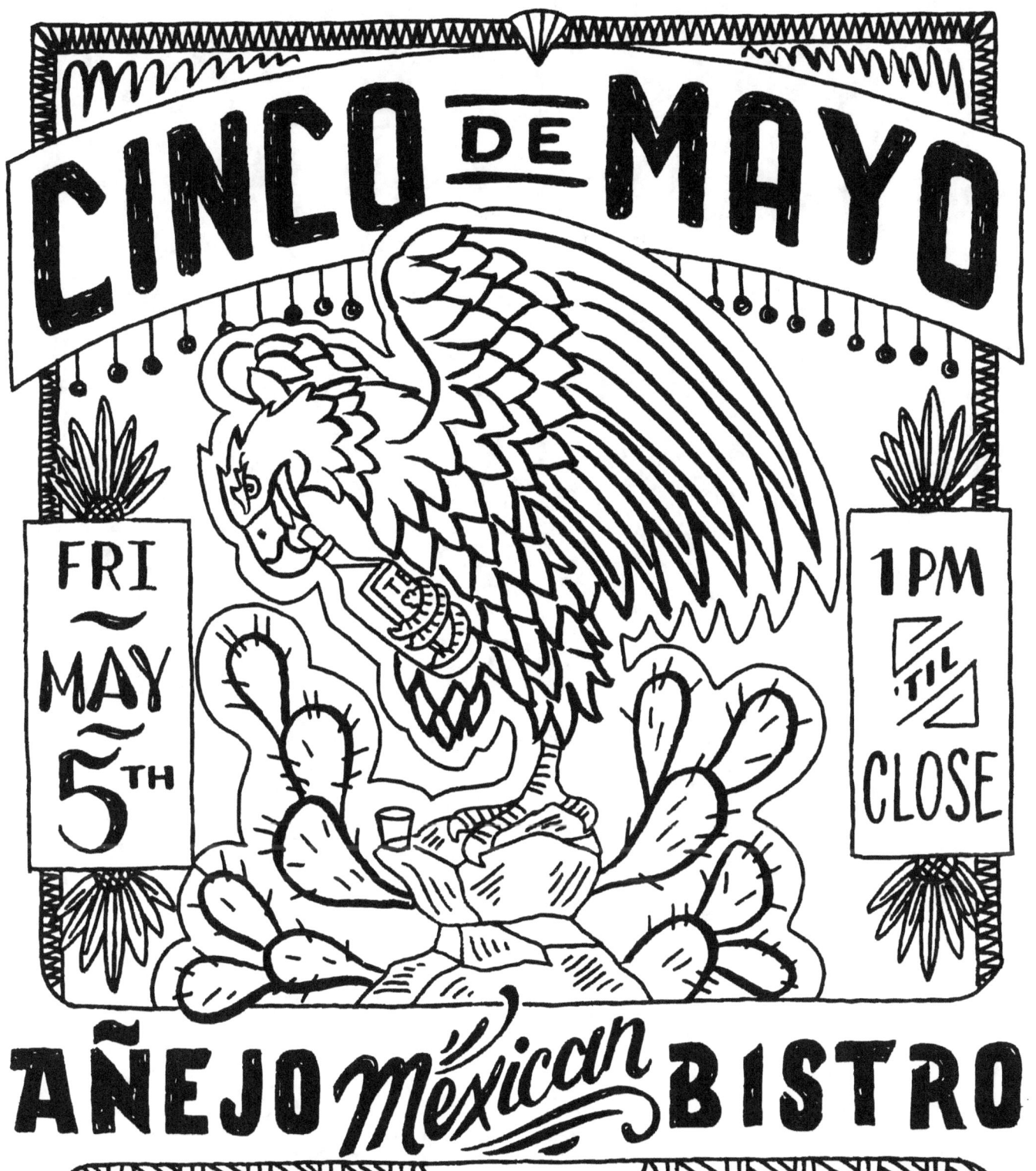

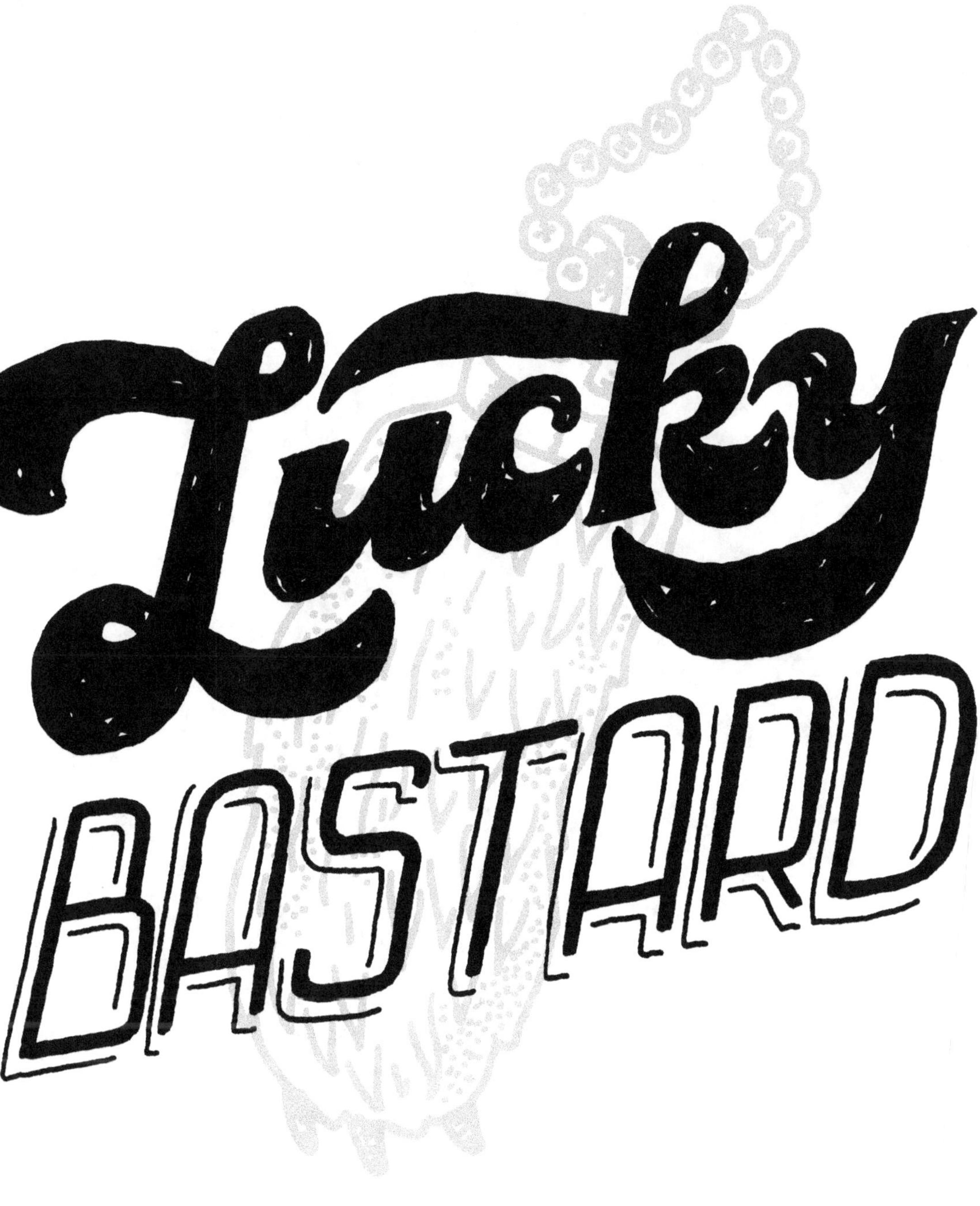

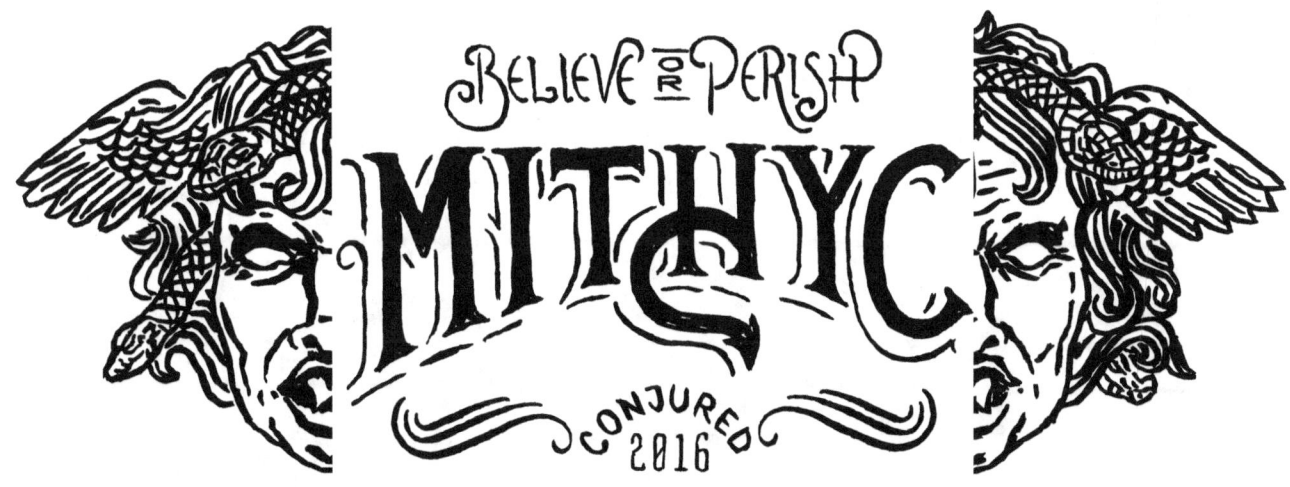

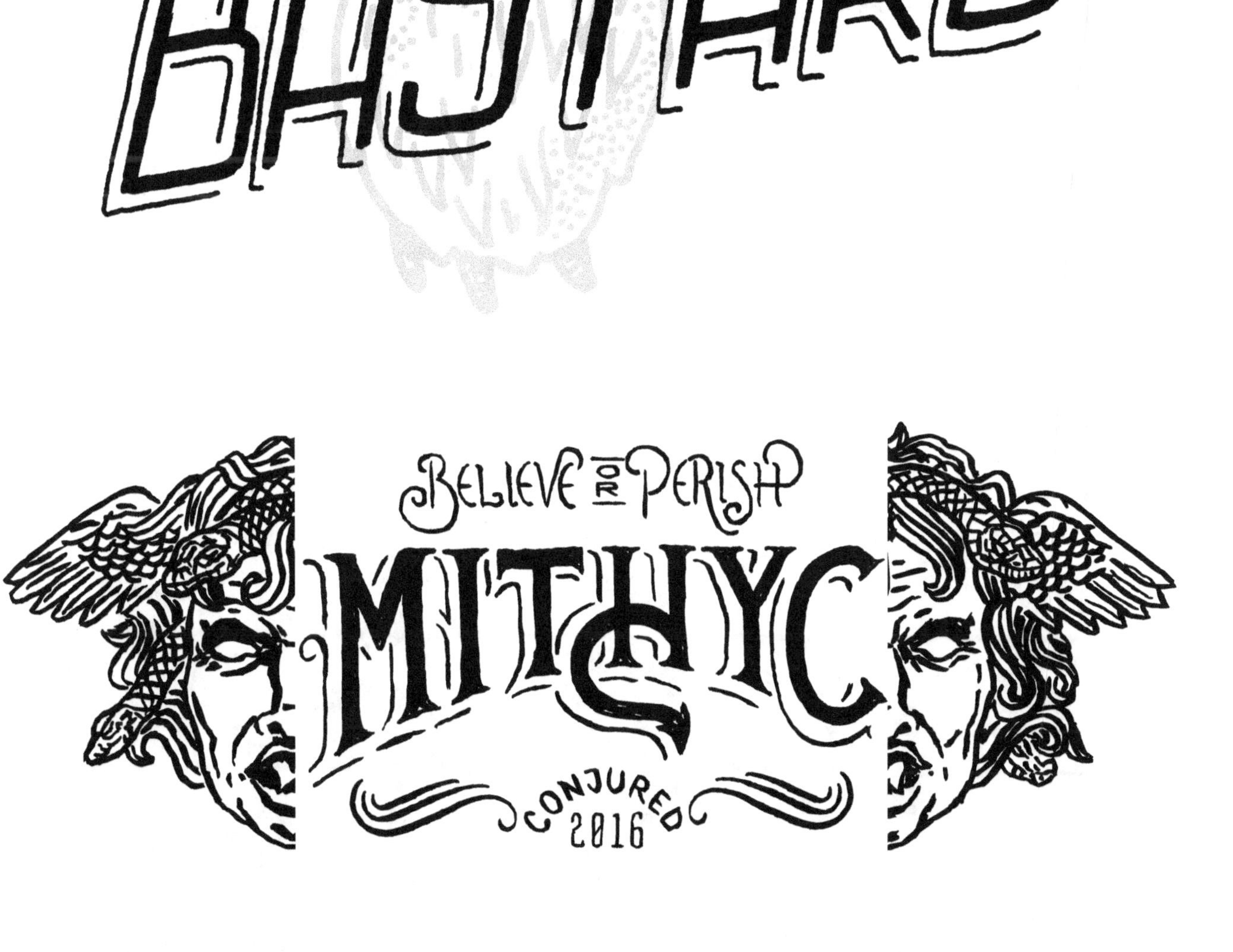

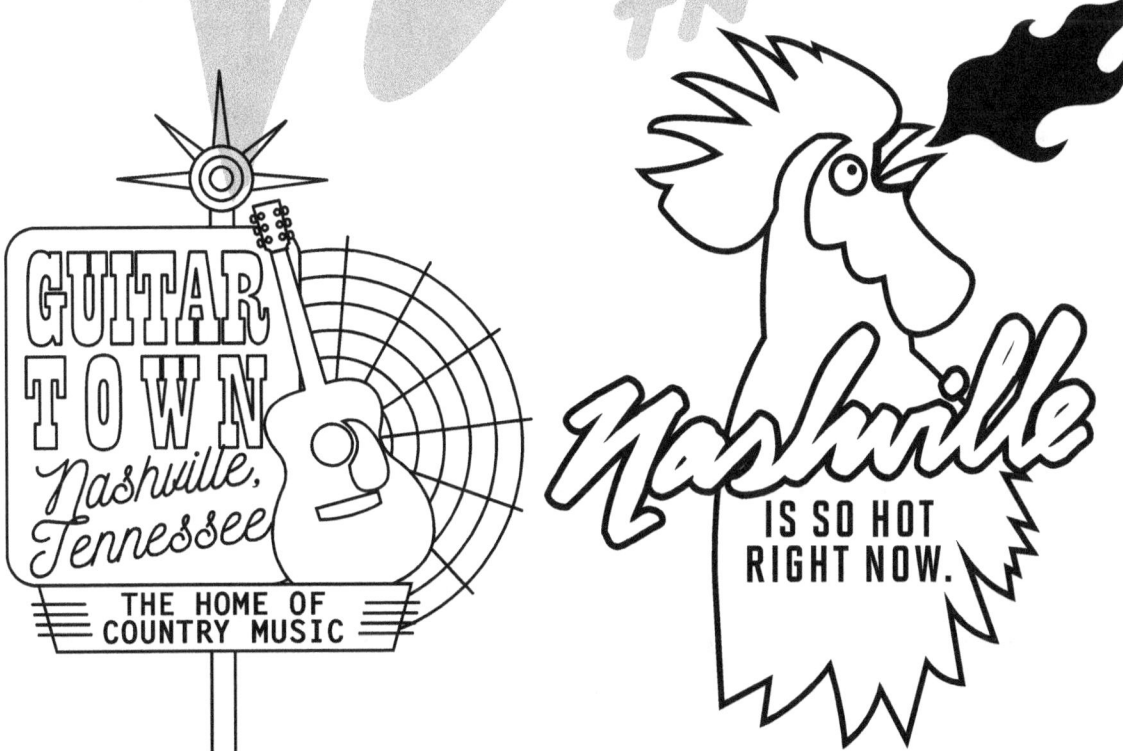

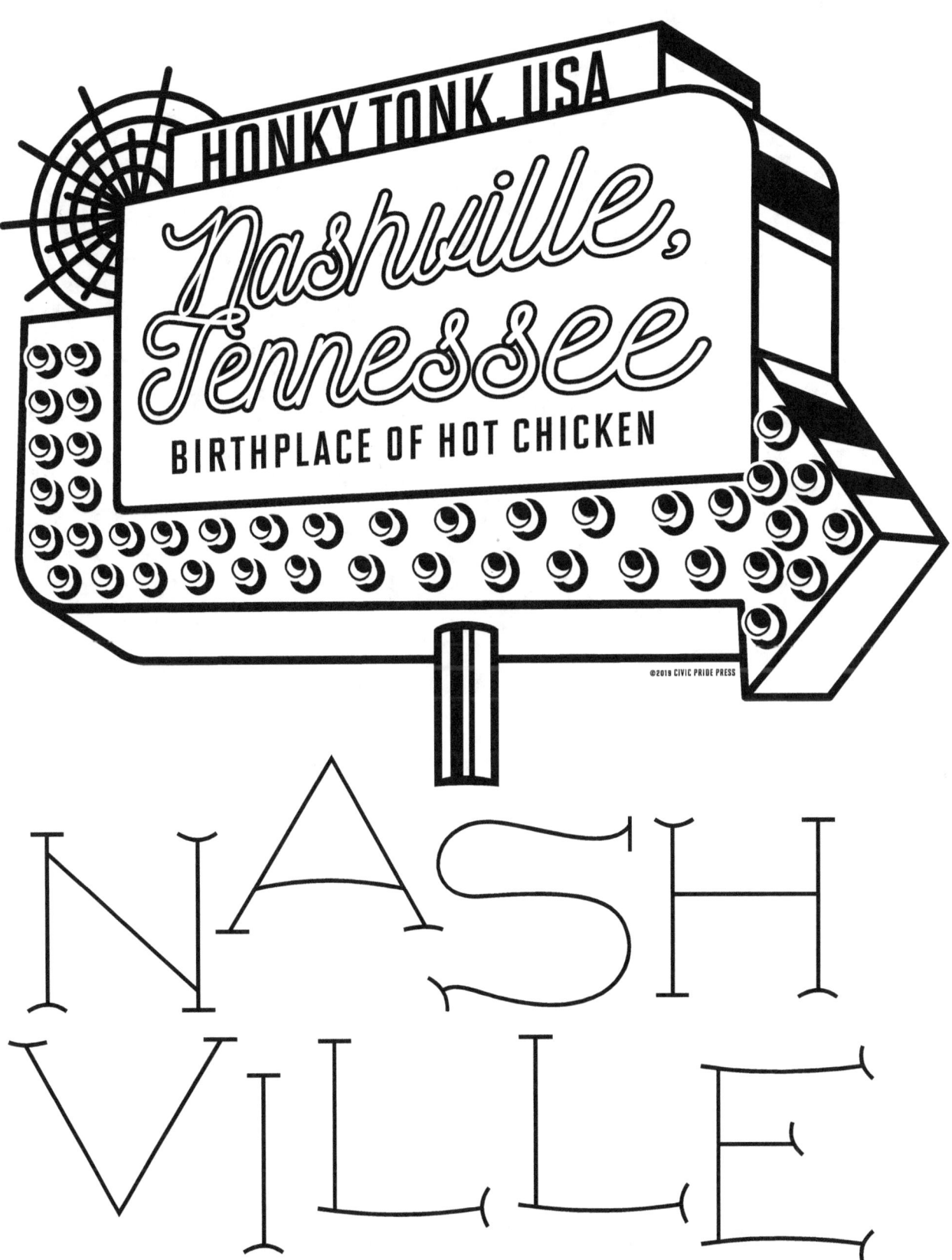

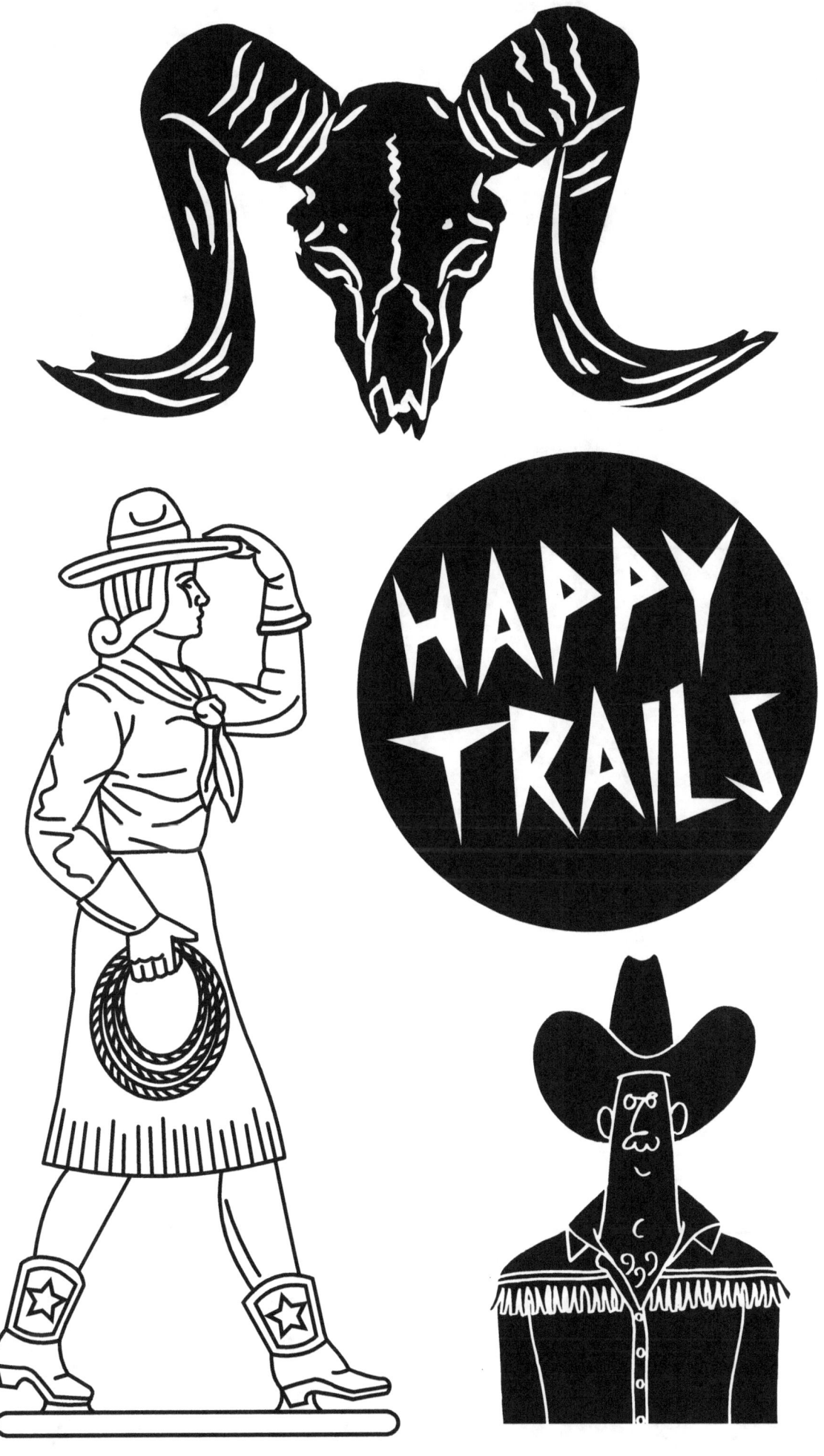

ABCDEFG
HIJKLMN
OPQRSTU
VWXYZ

STAGECOACH
ANTICS
DISPLAY FONT

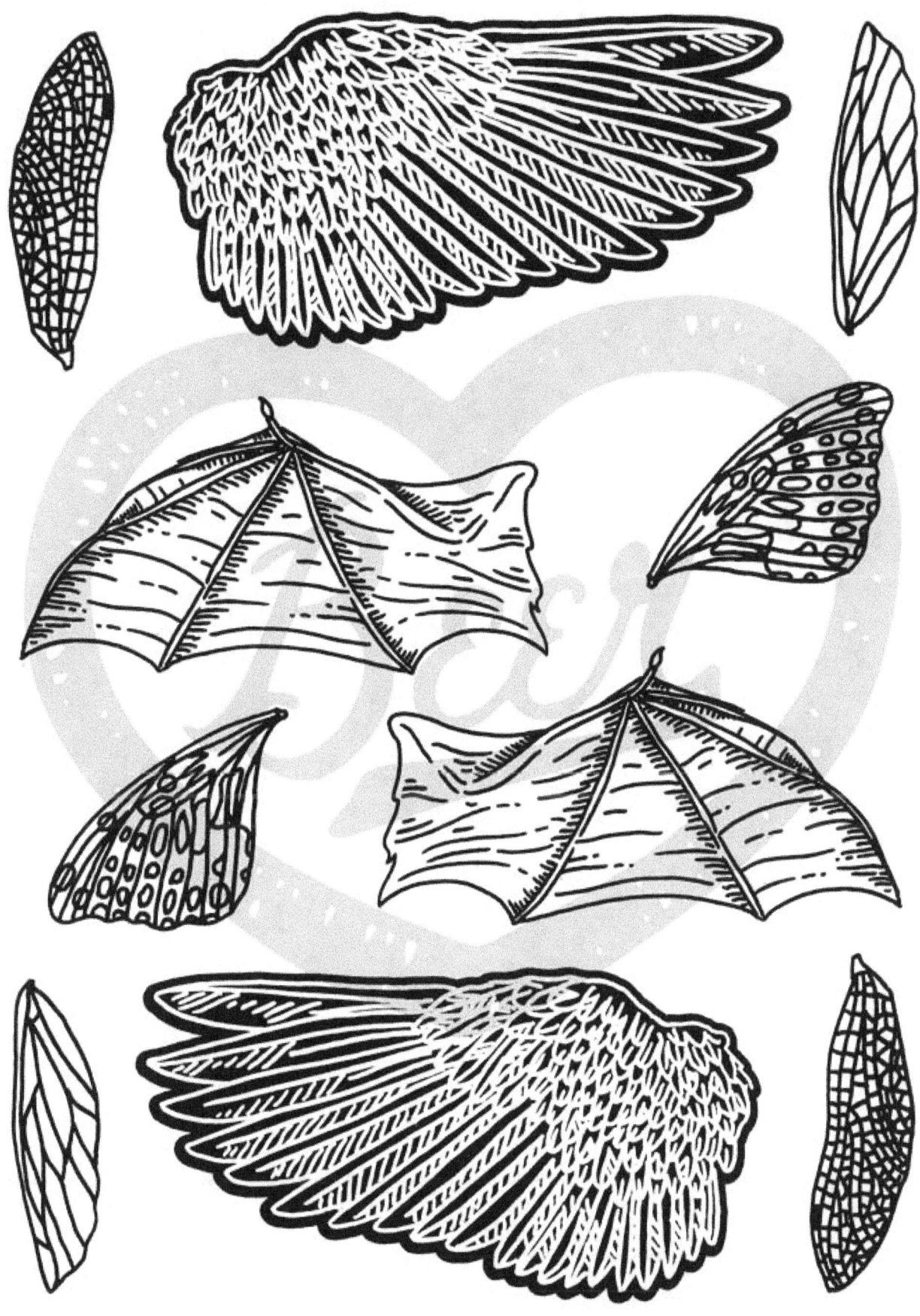

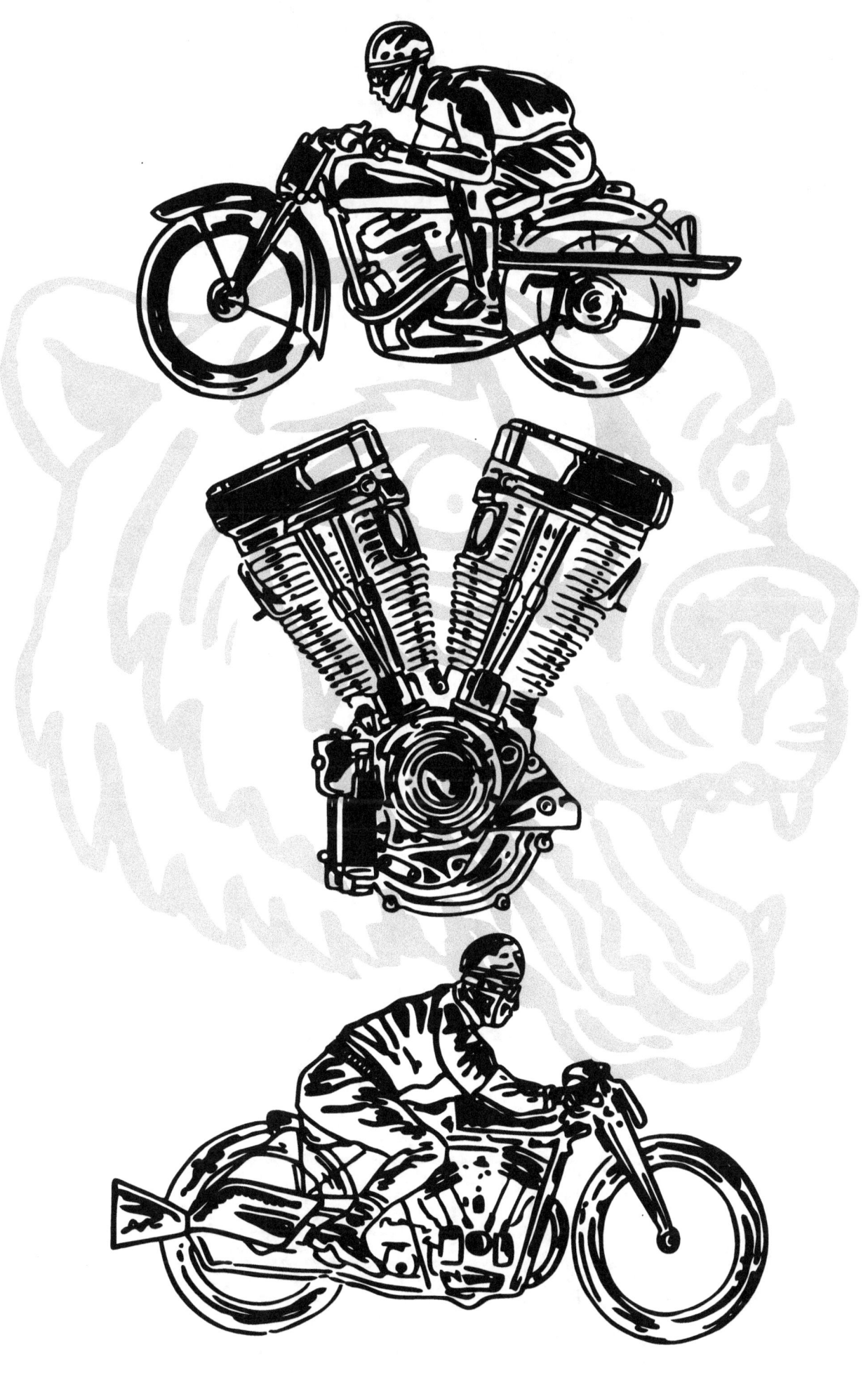

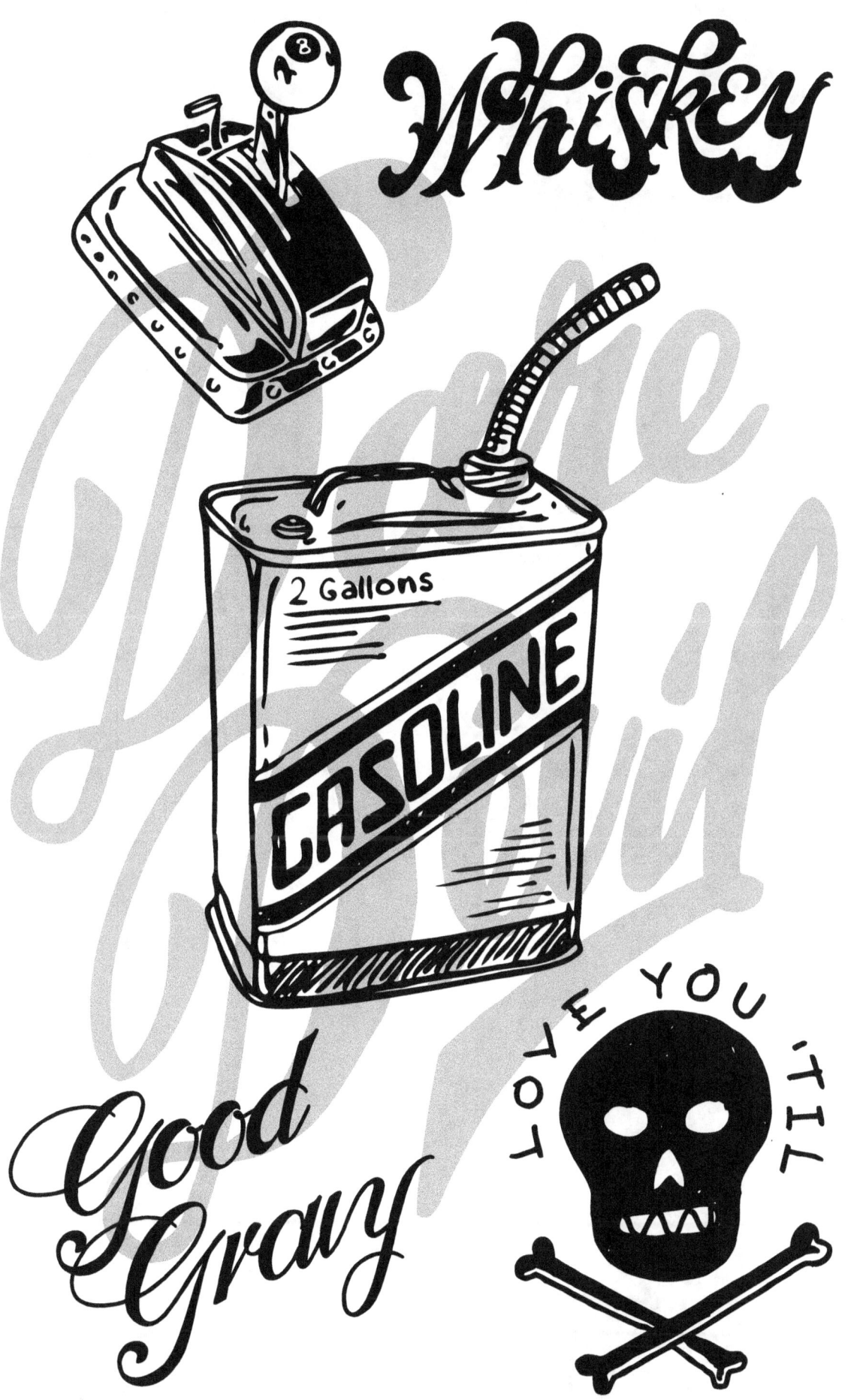

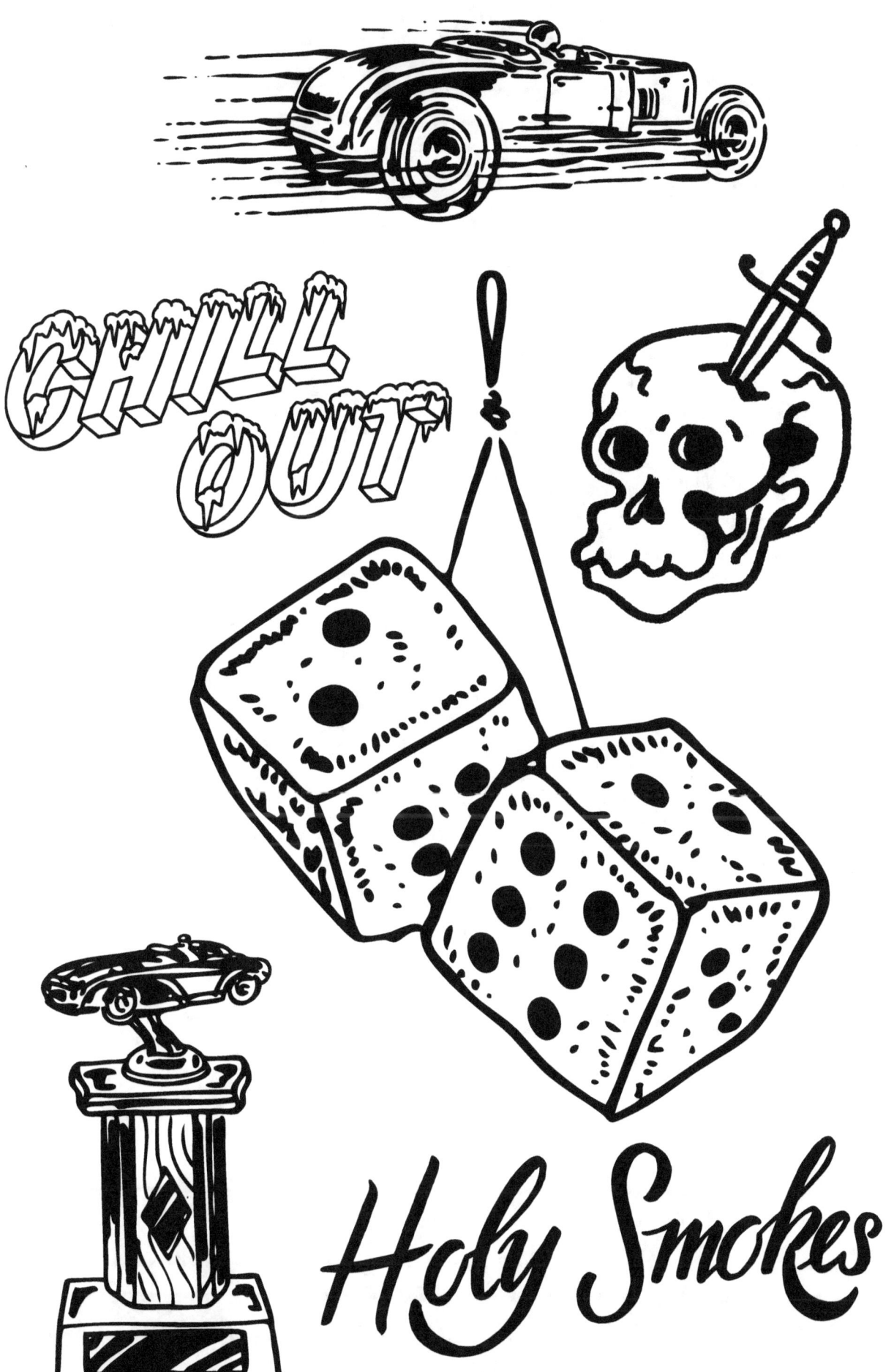

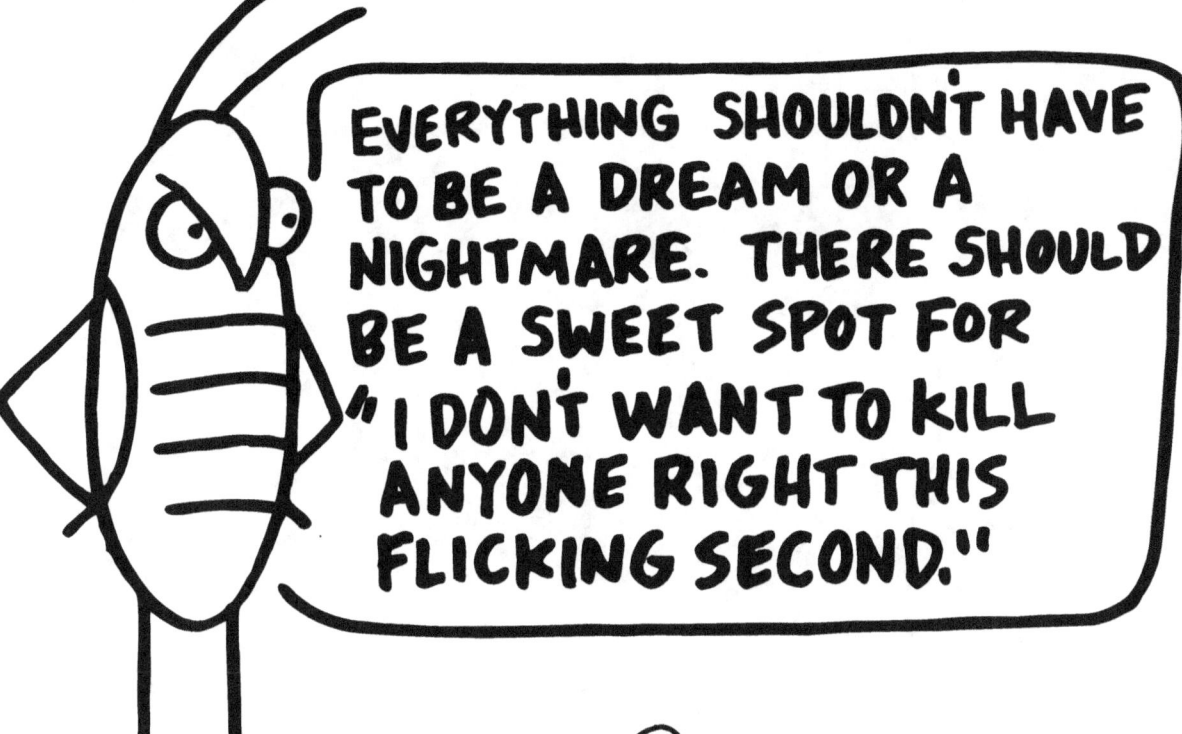

THE RARE PIGEON™

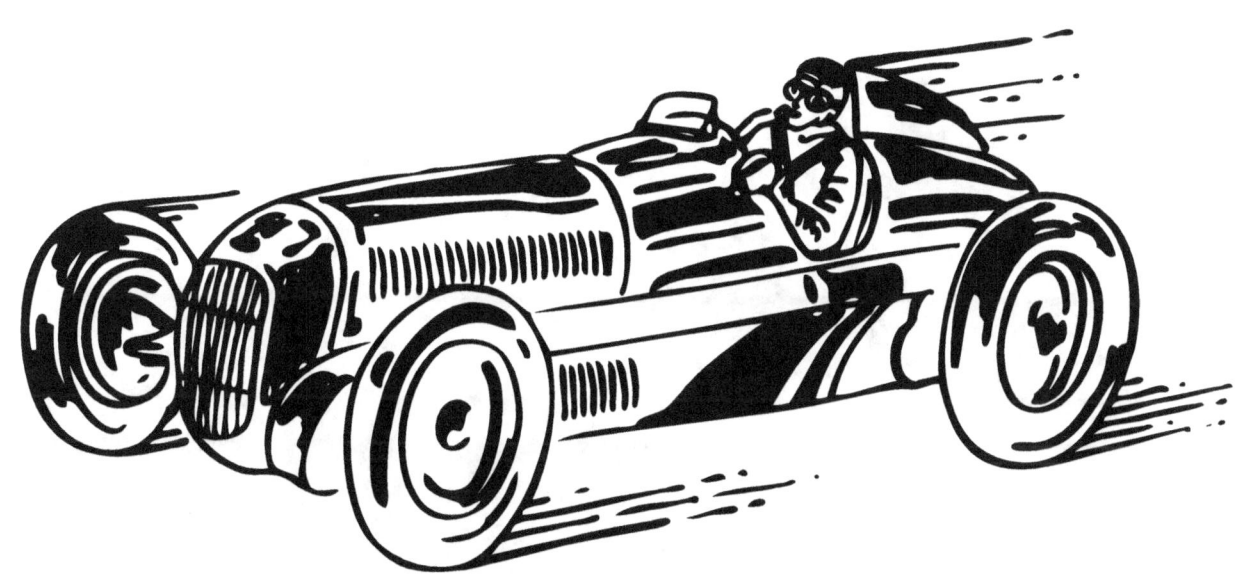

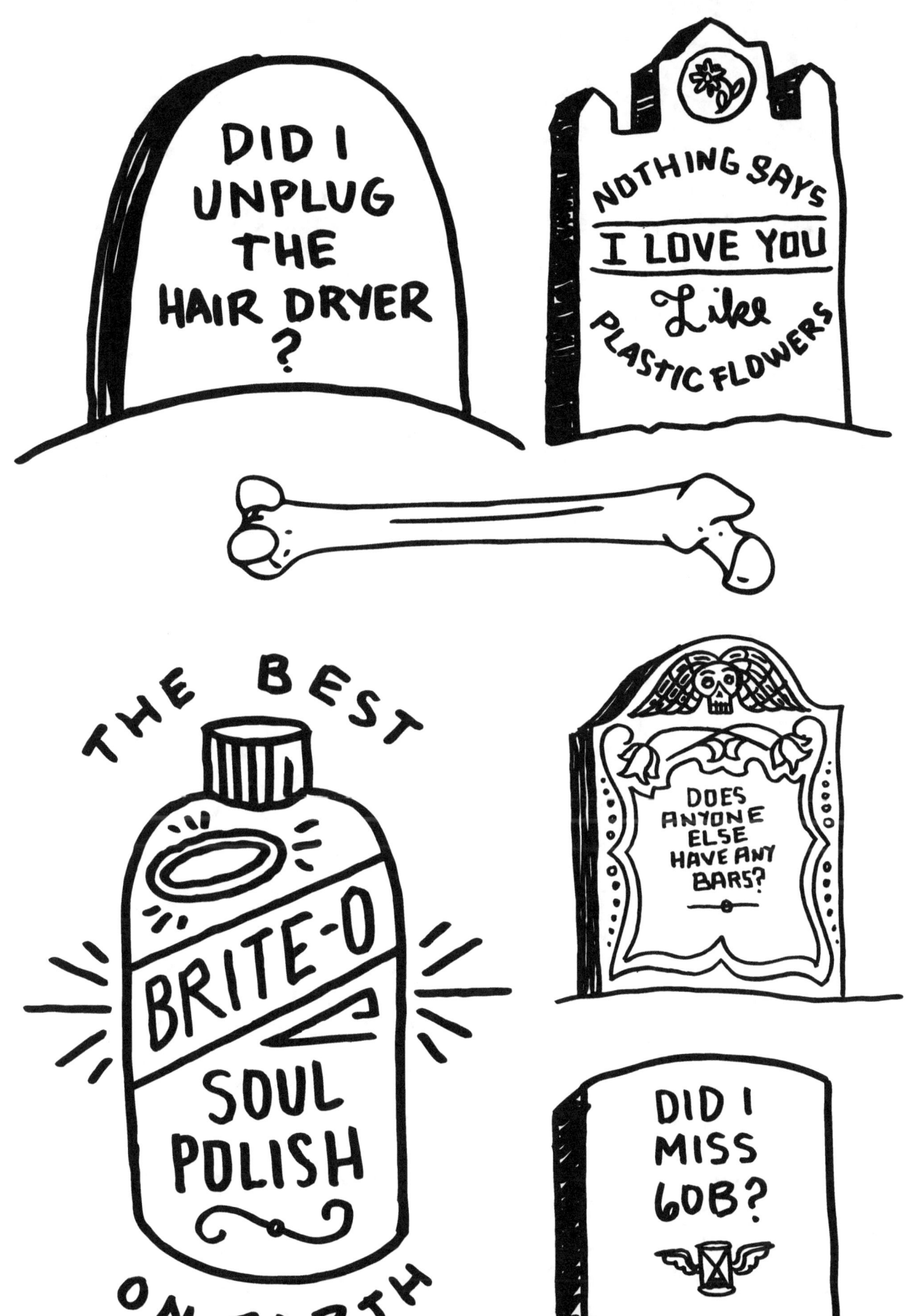

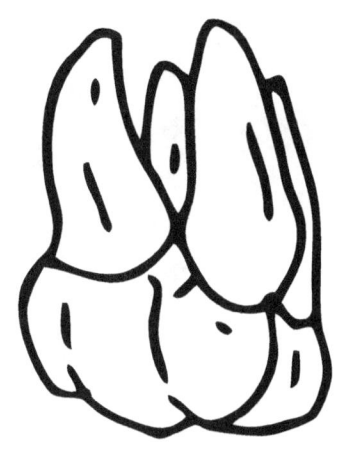
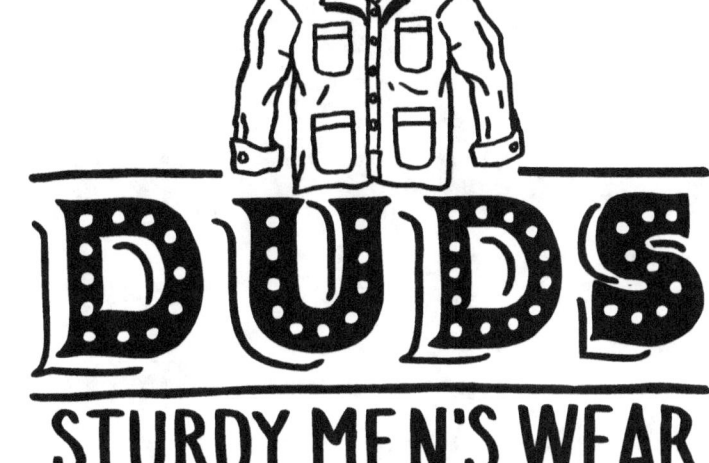
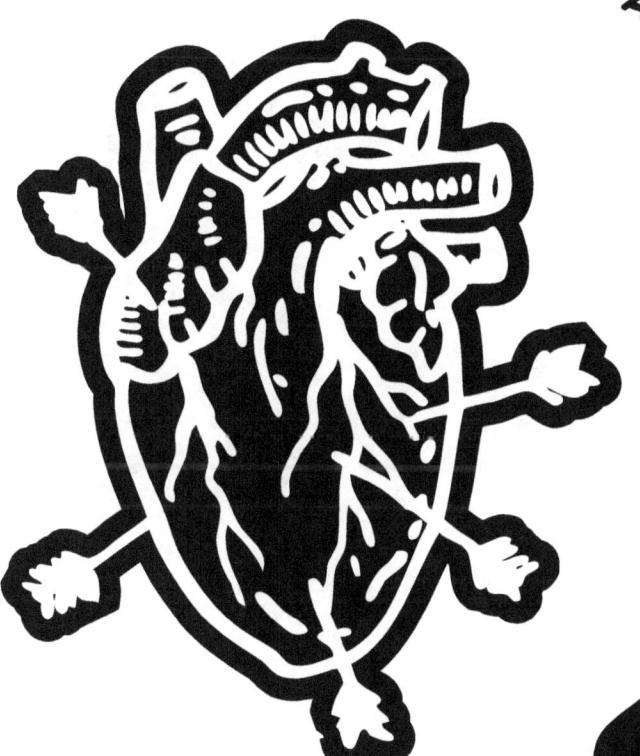
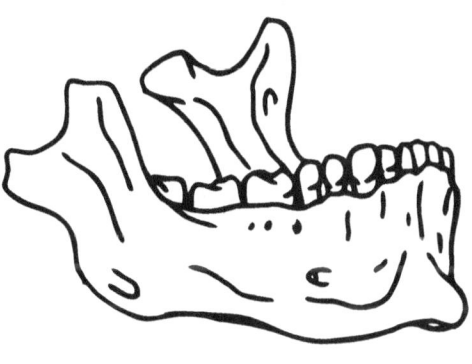
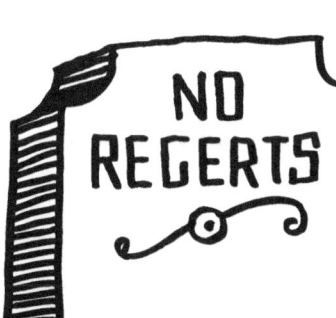
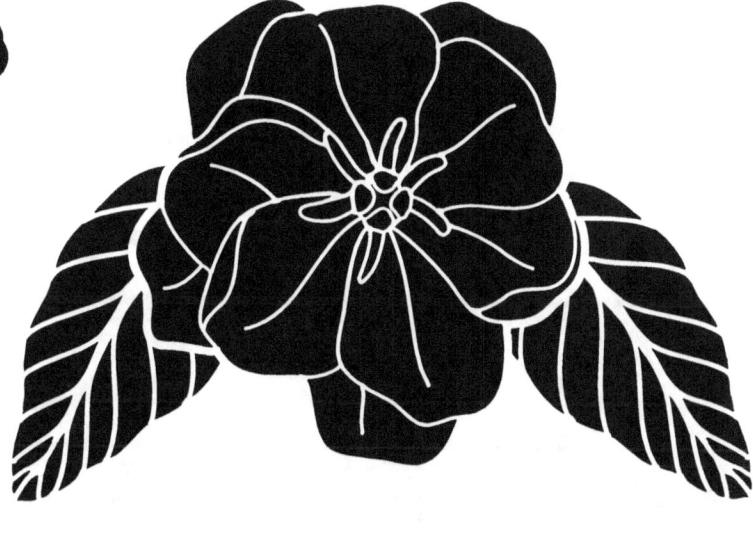

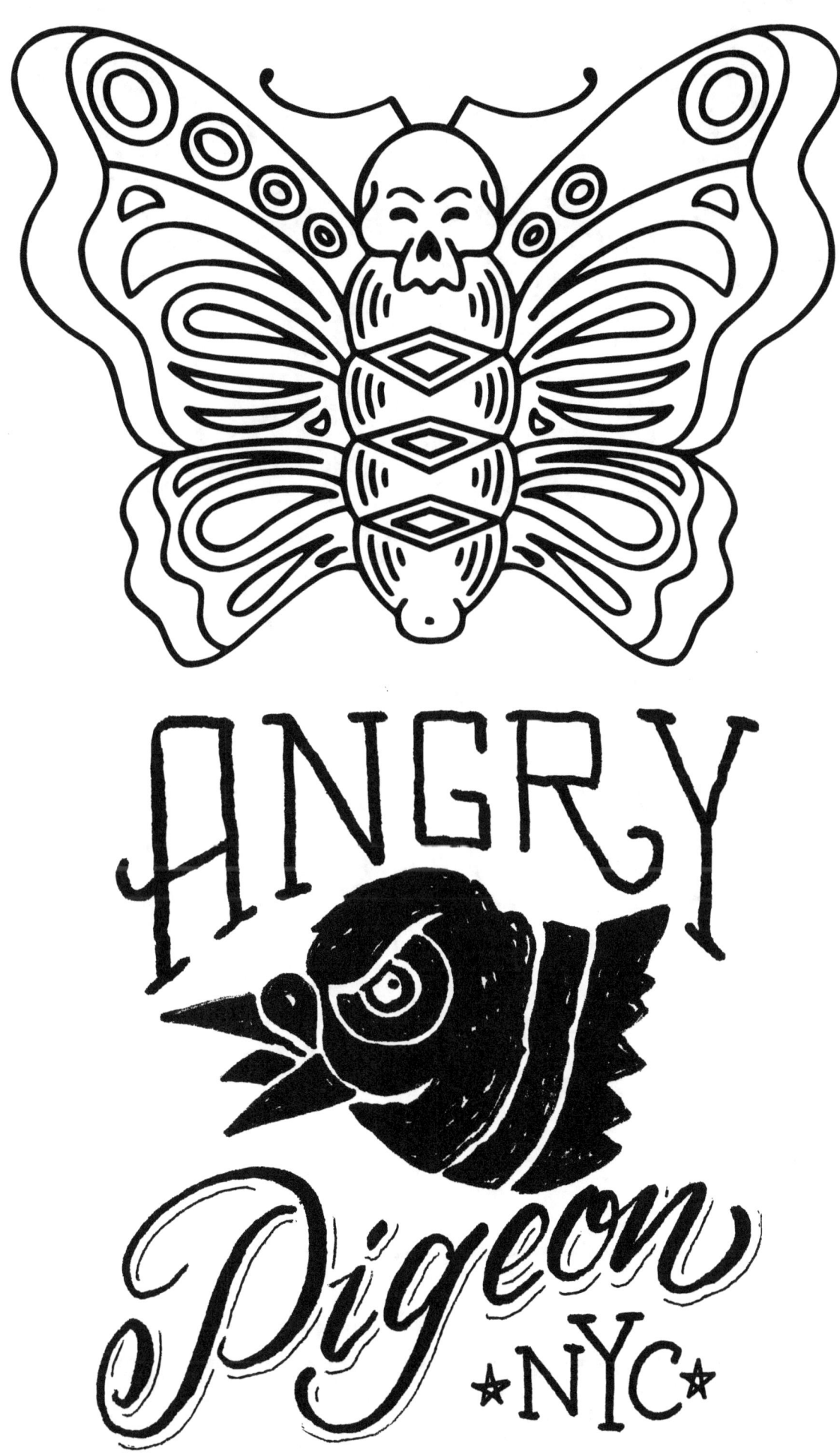

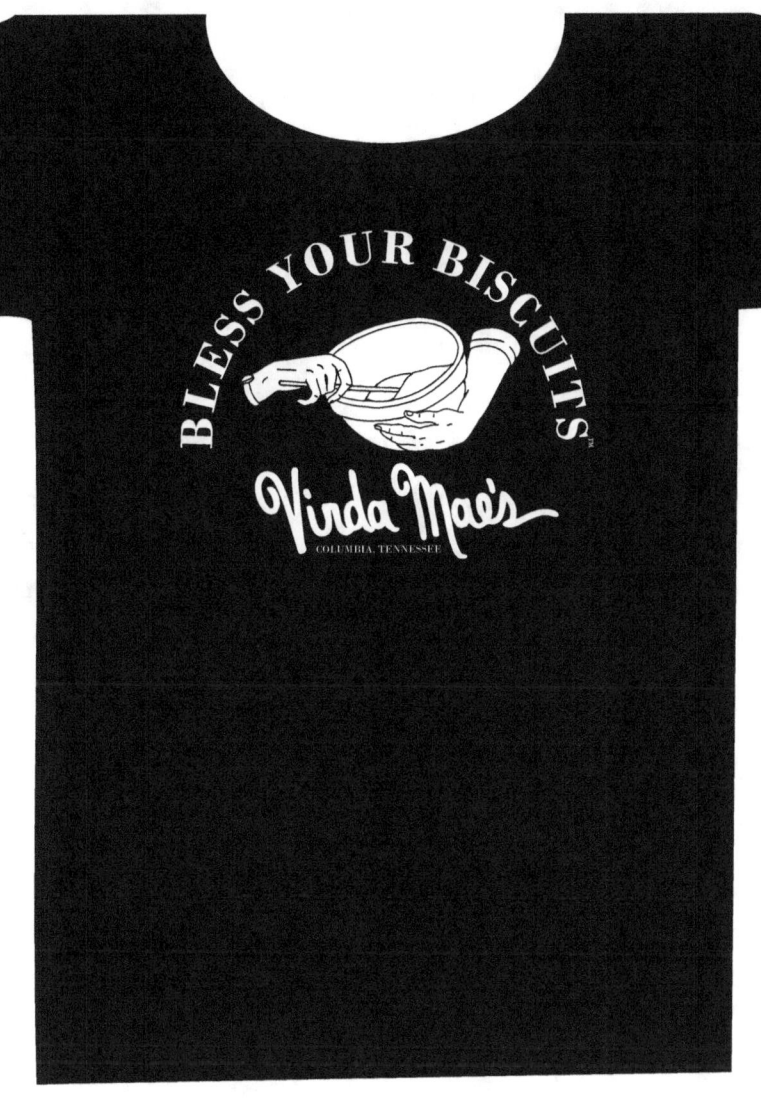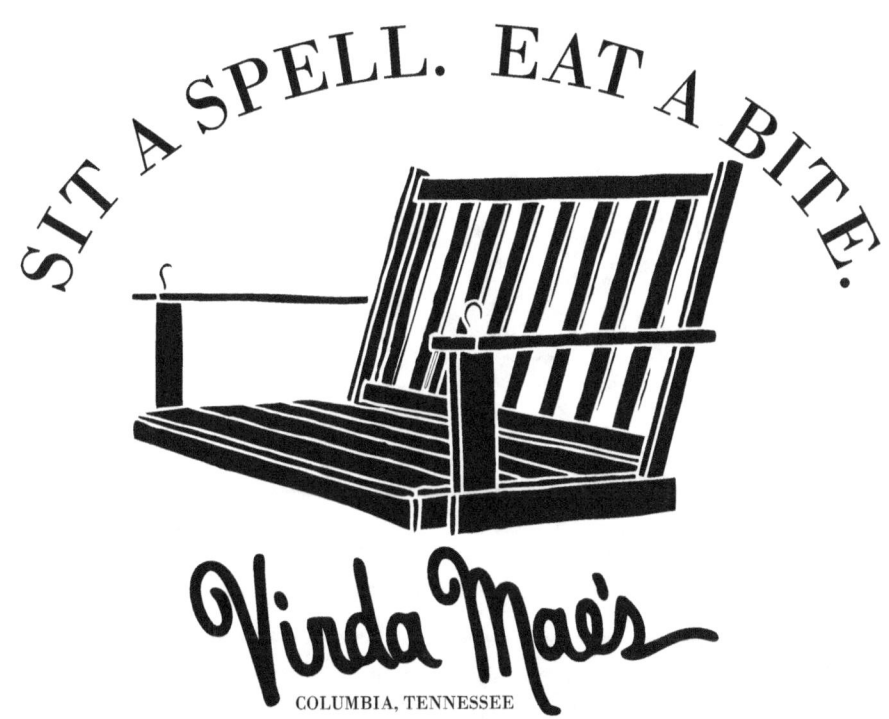

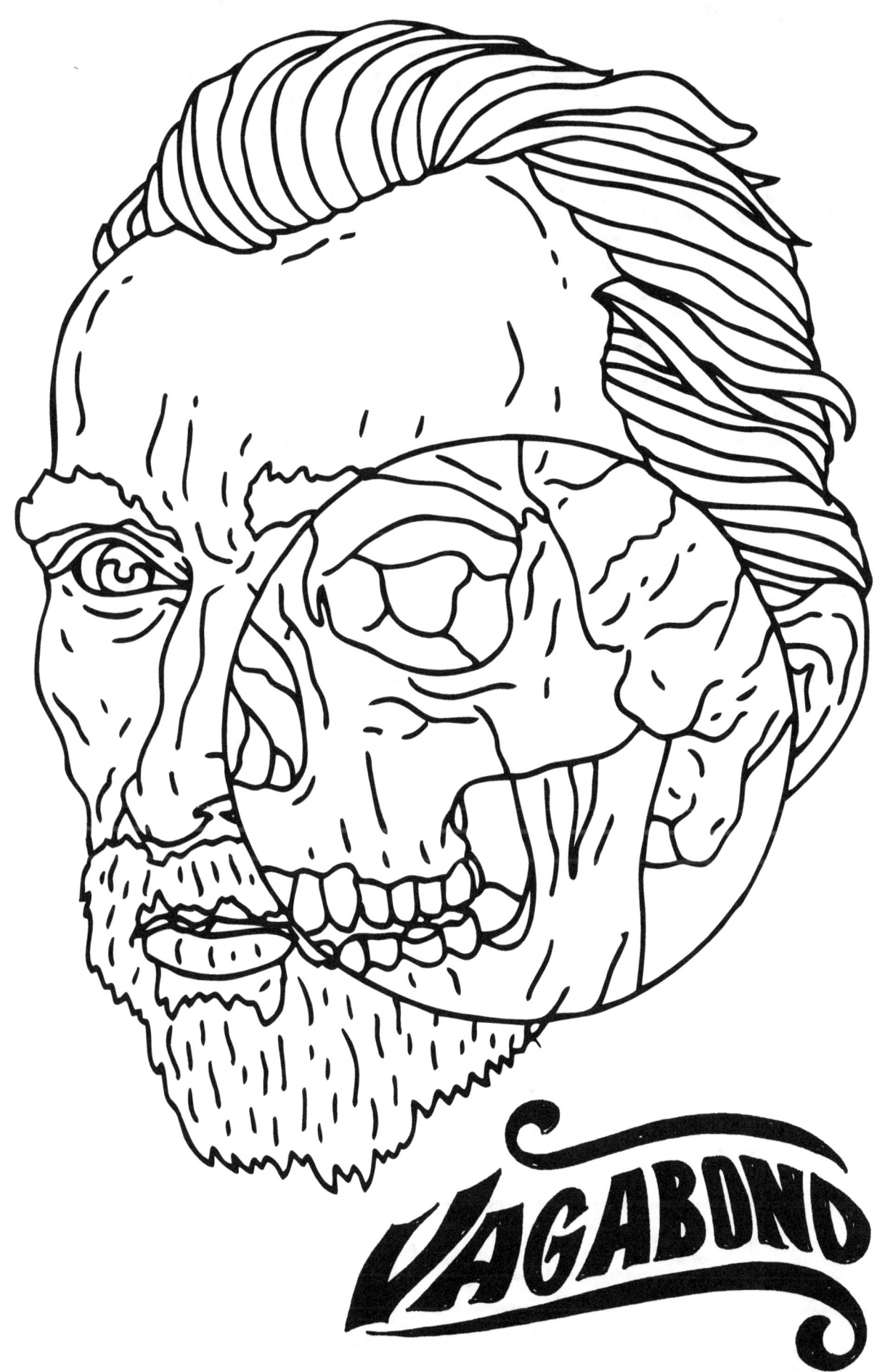

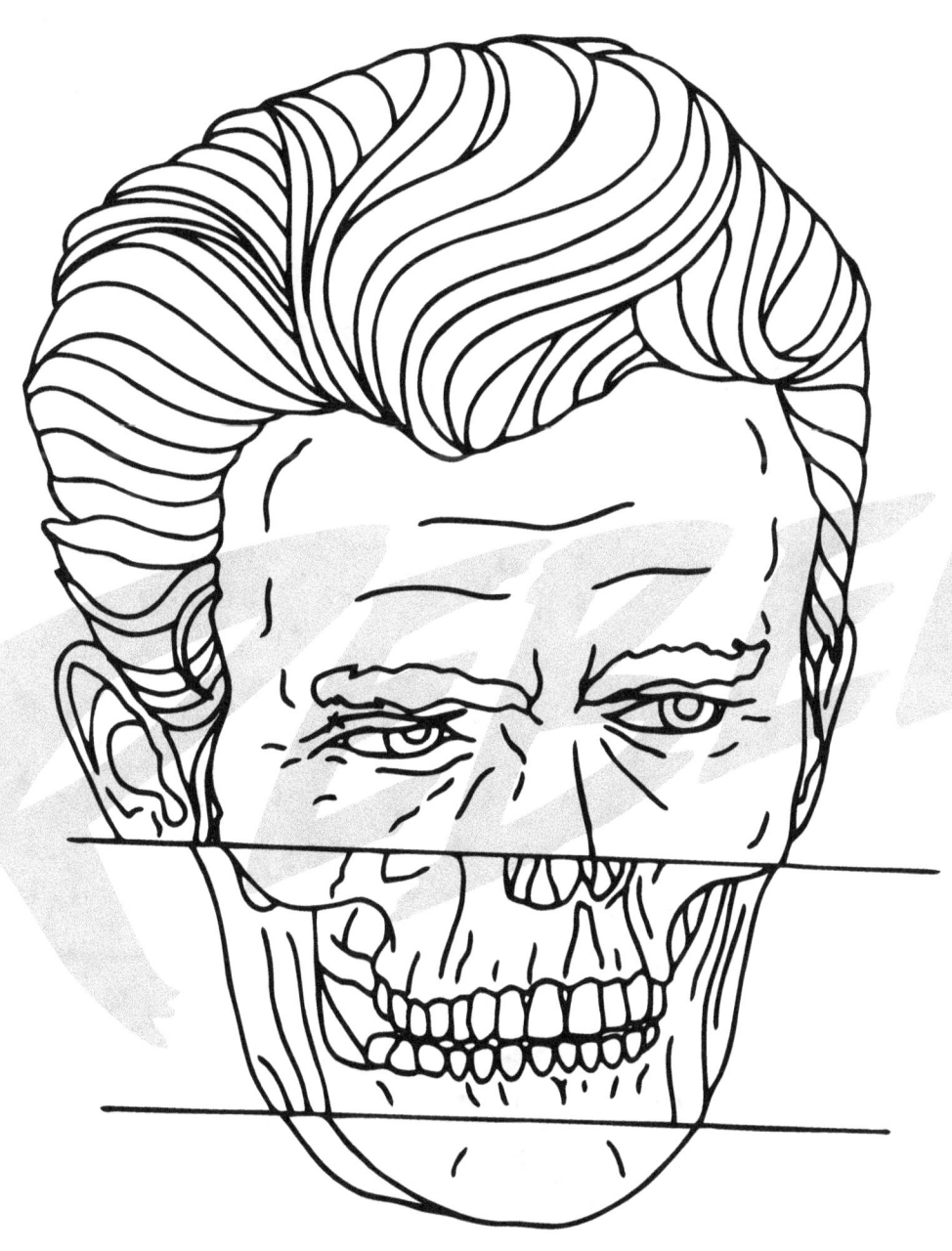

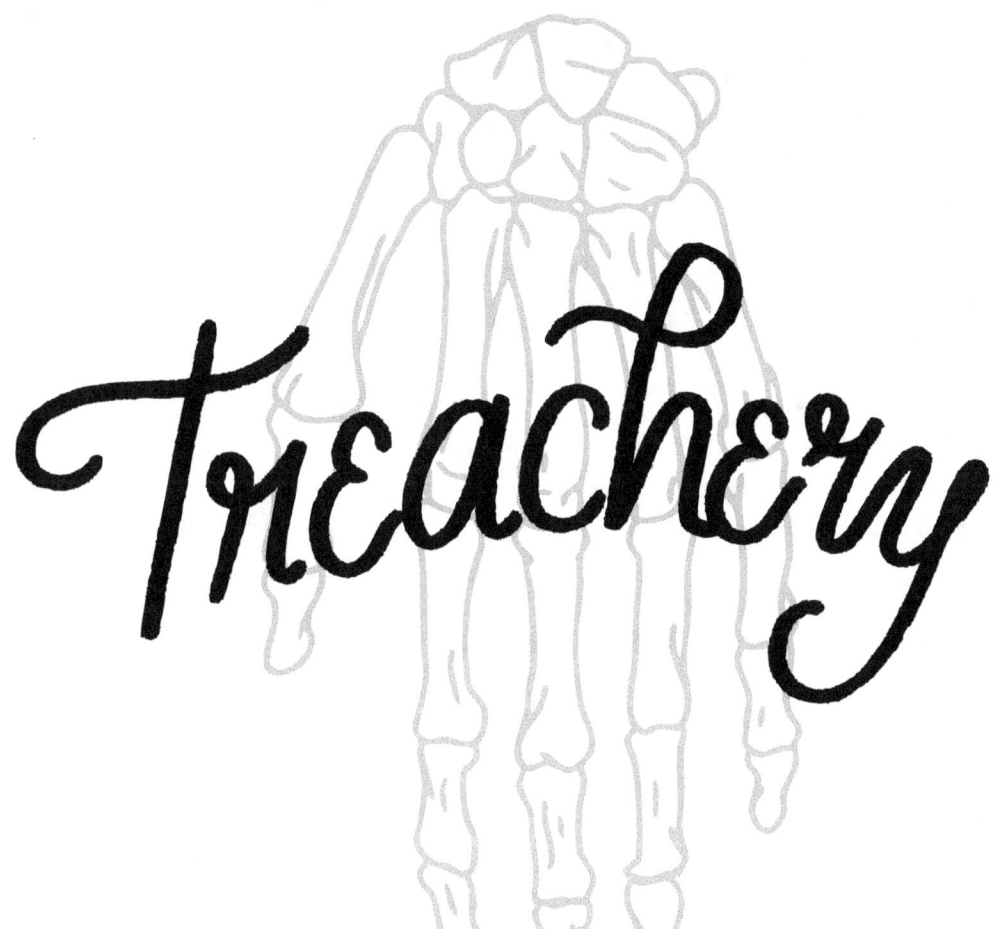

Snake Eyes

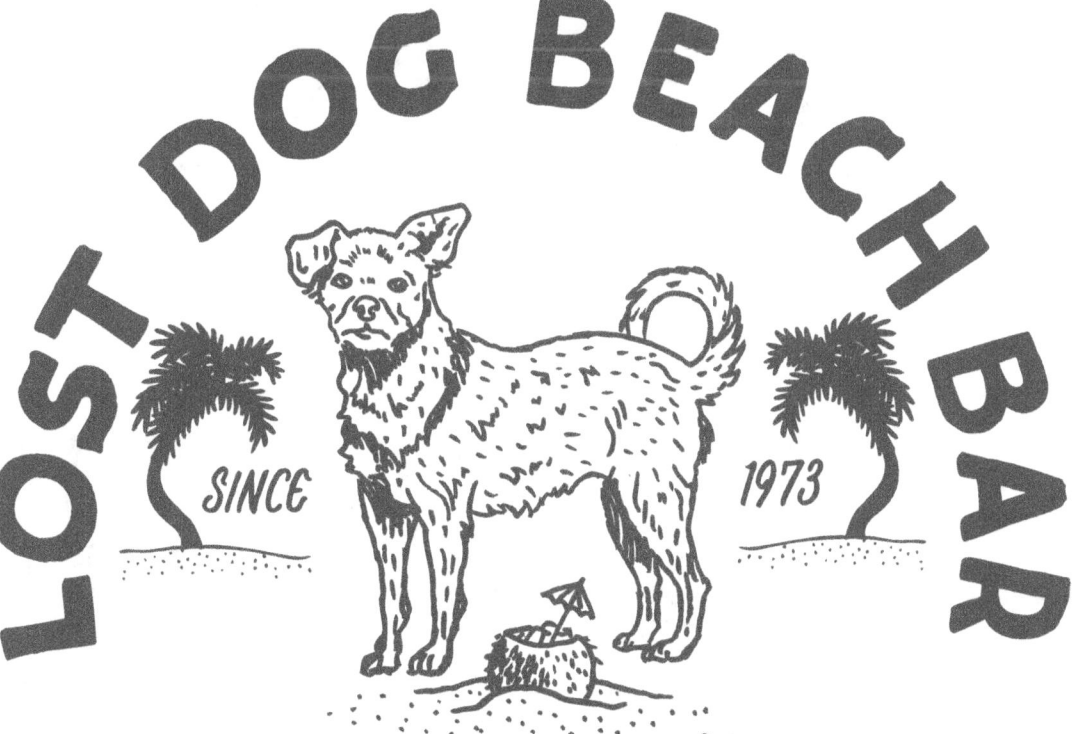

LOST DOG BEACH BAR

SINCE 1973

The best place to be a stray.

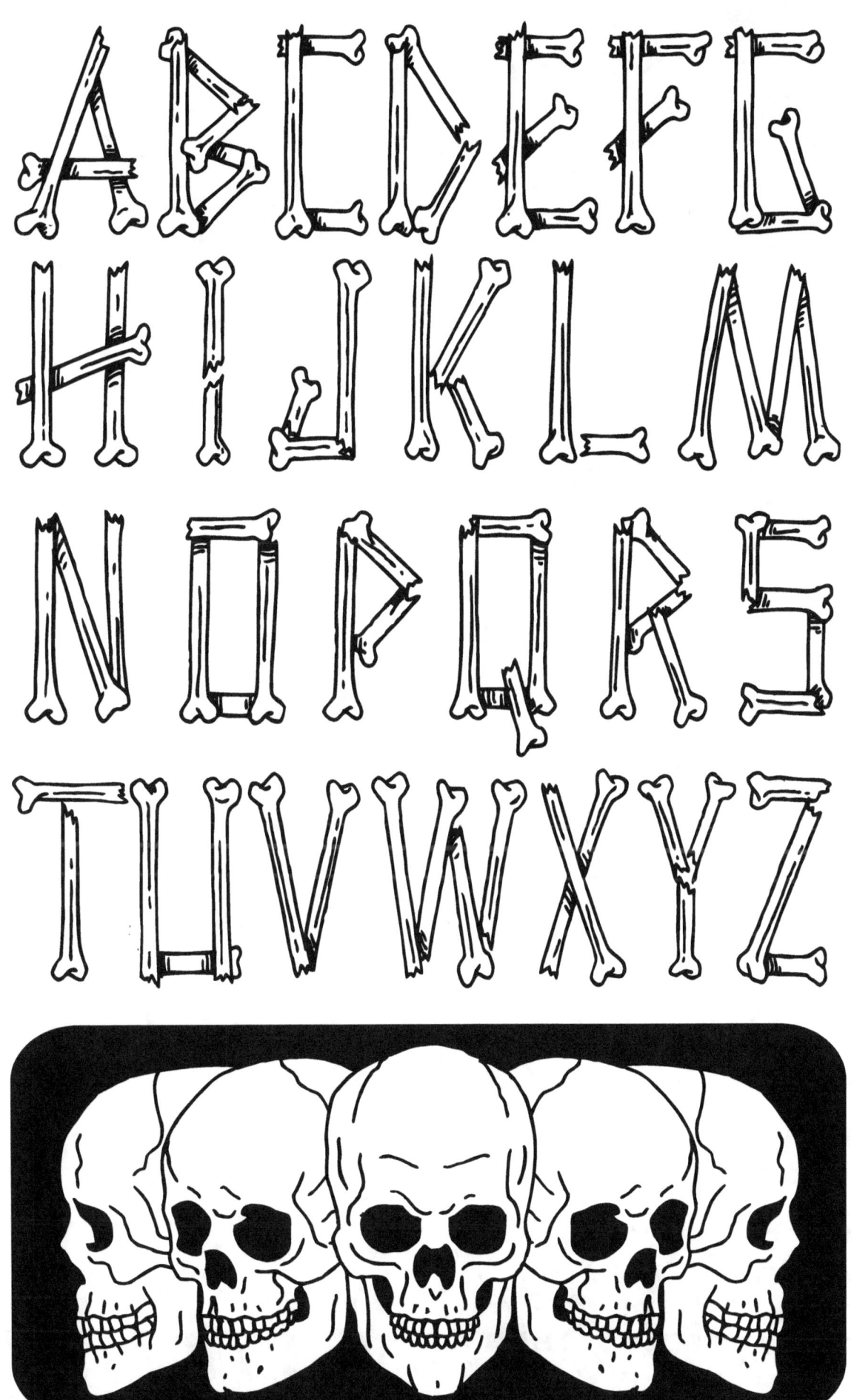

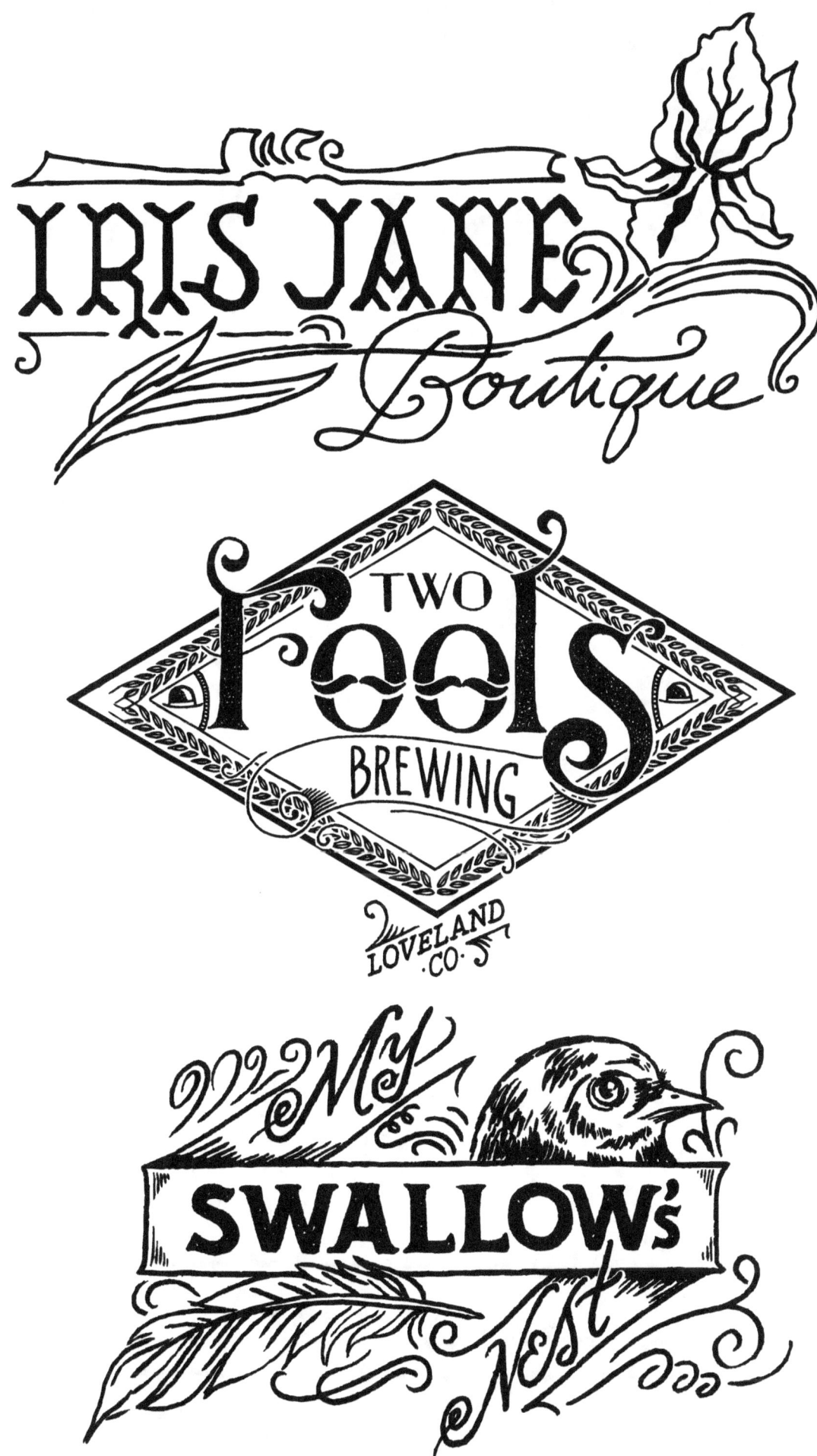

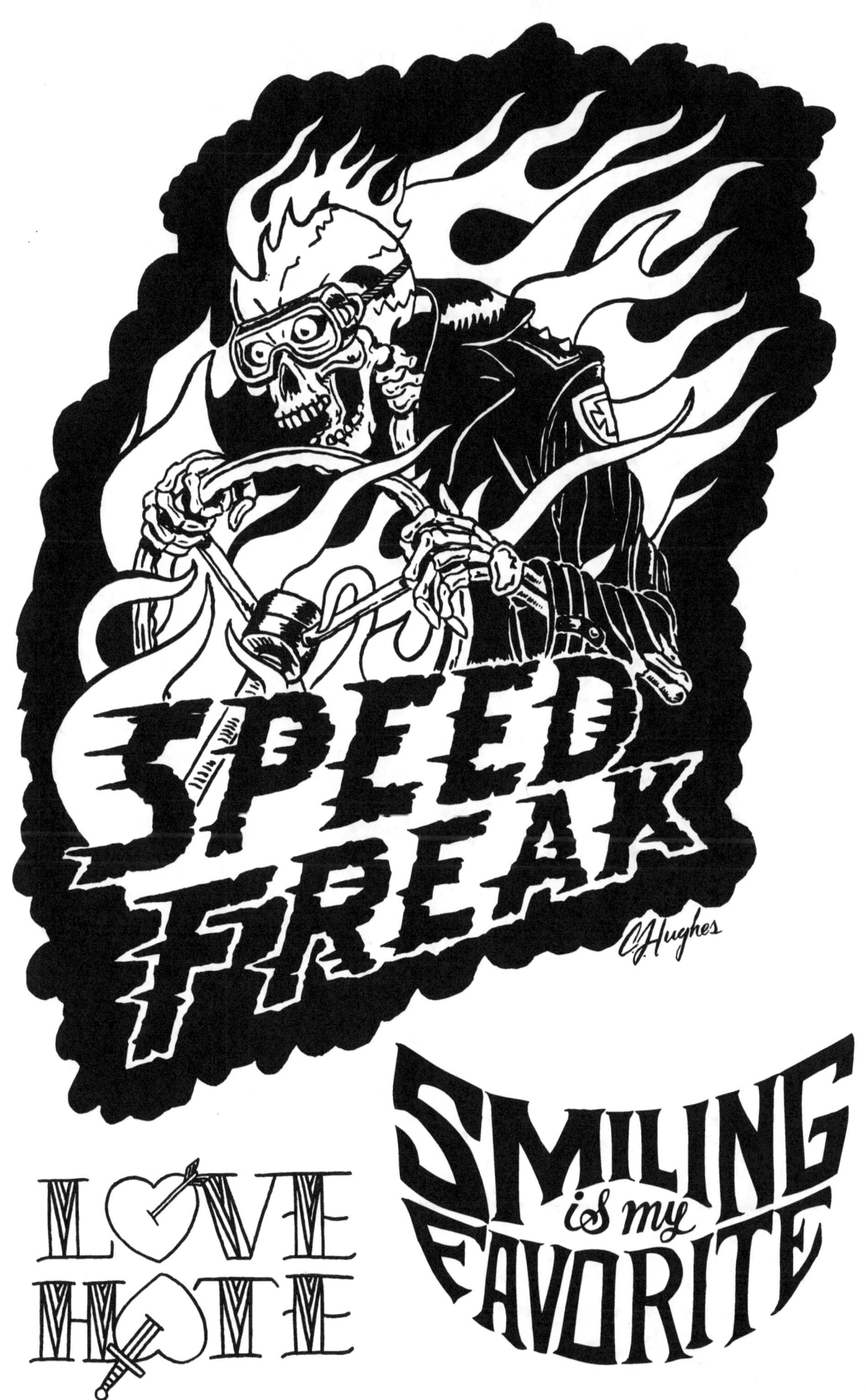

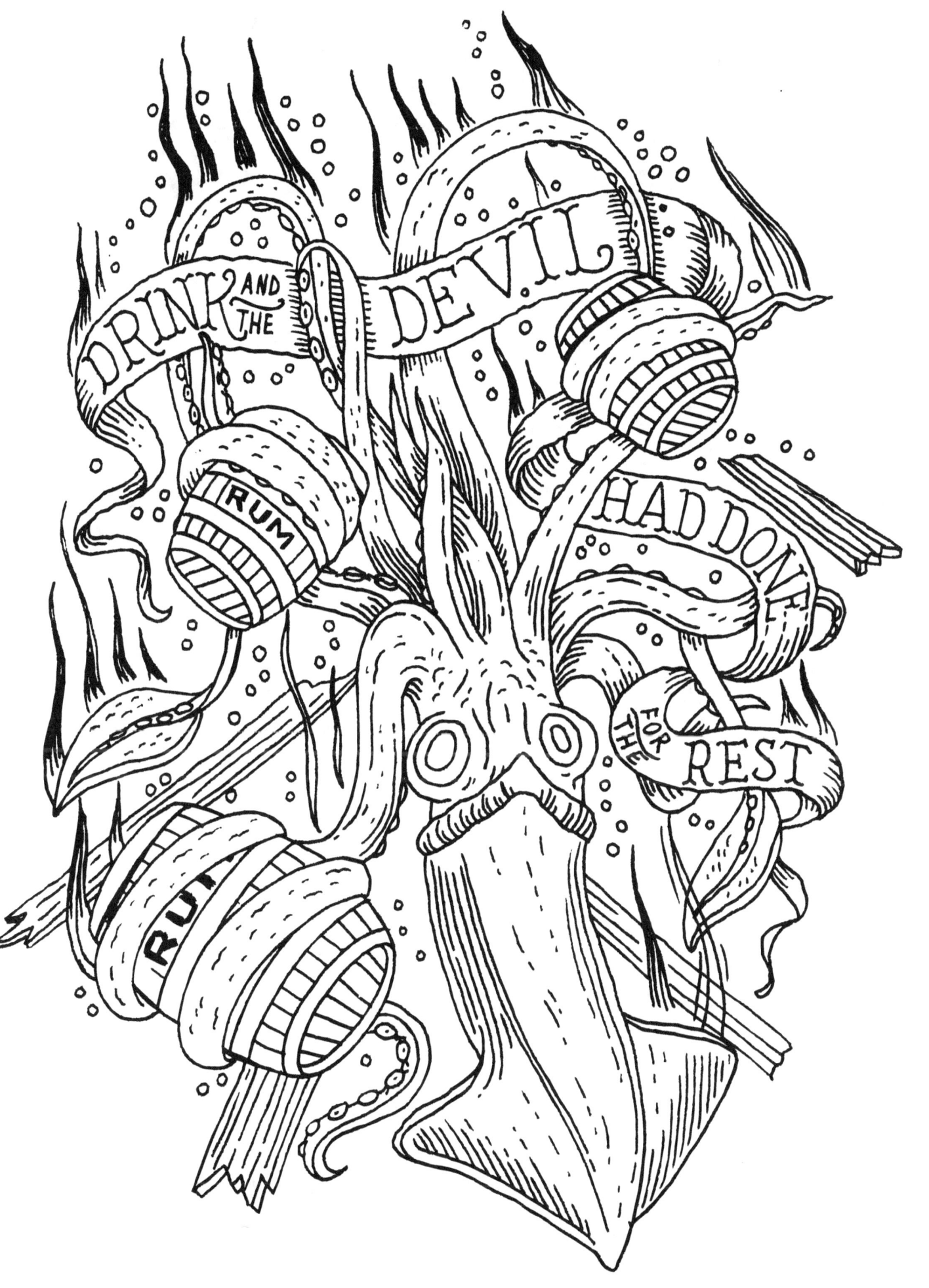

ABCDEFG
HIJKLMN
OPQRSTU
VWXYZ

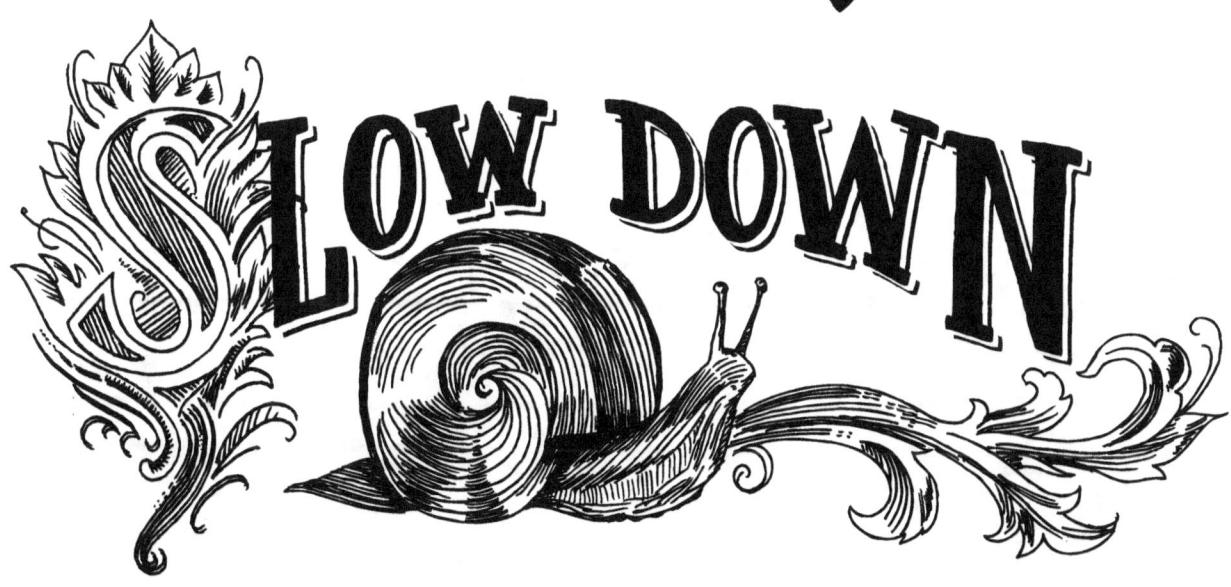

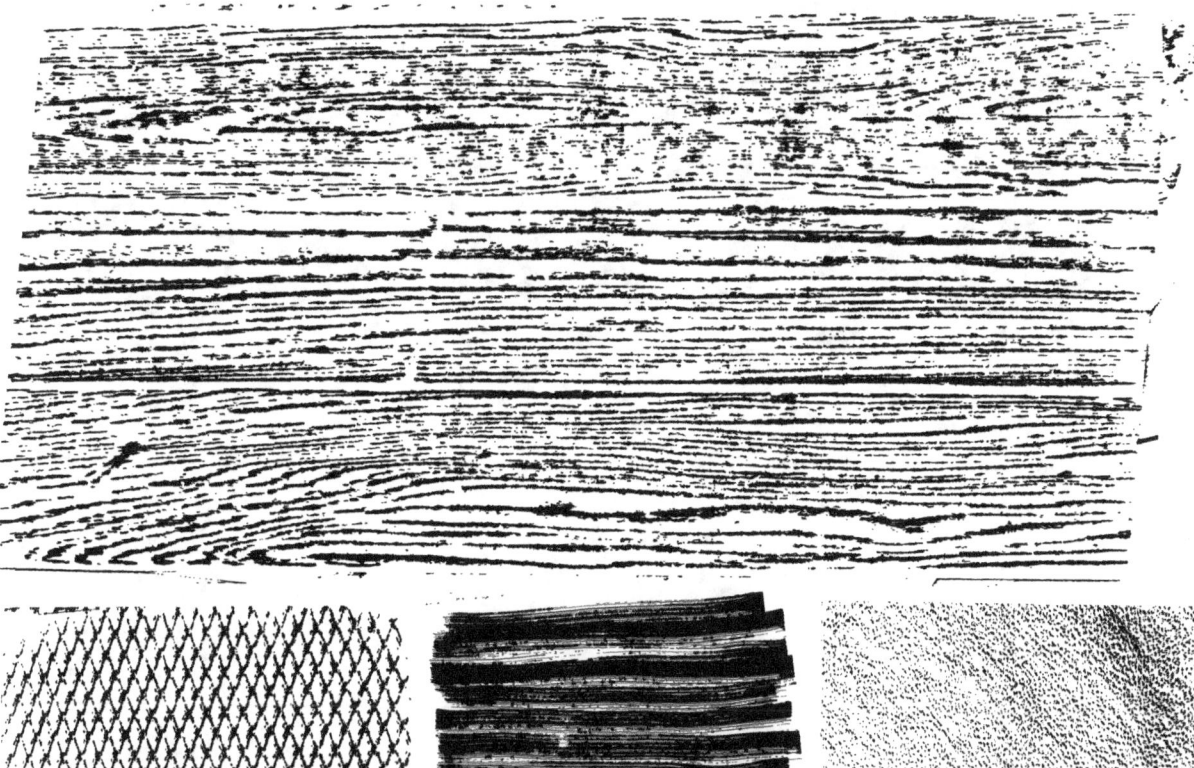
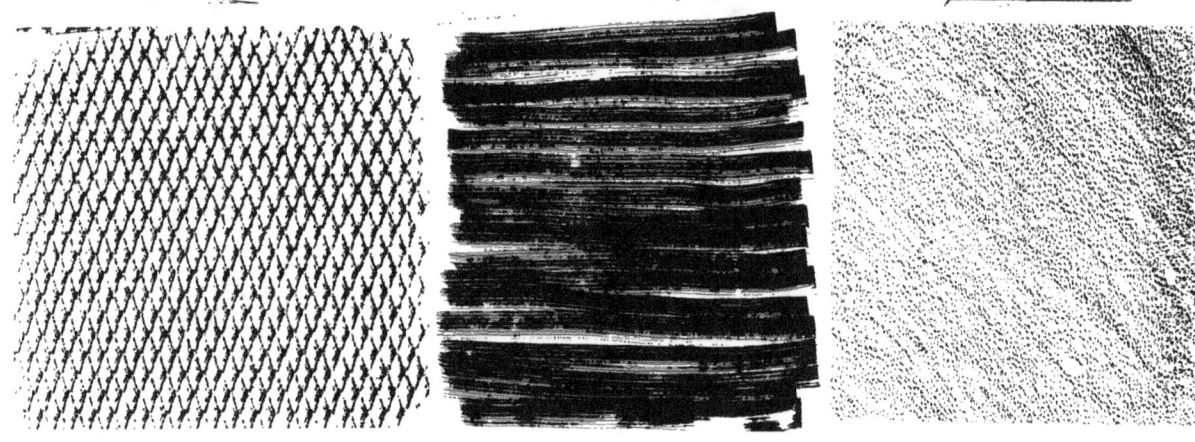
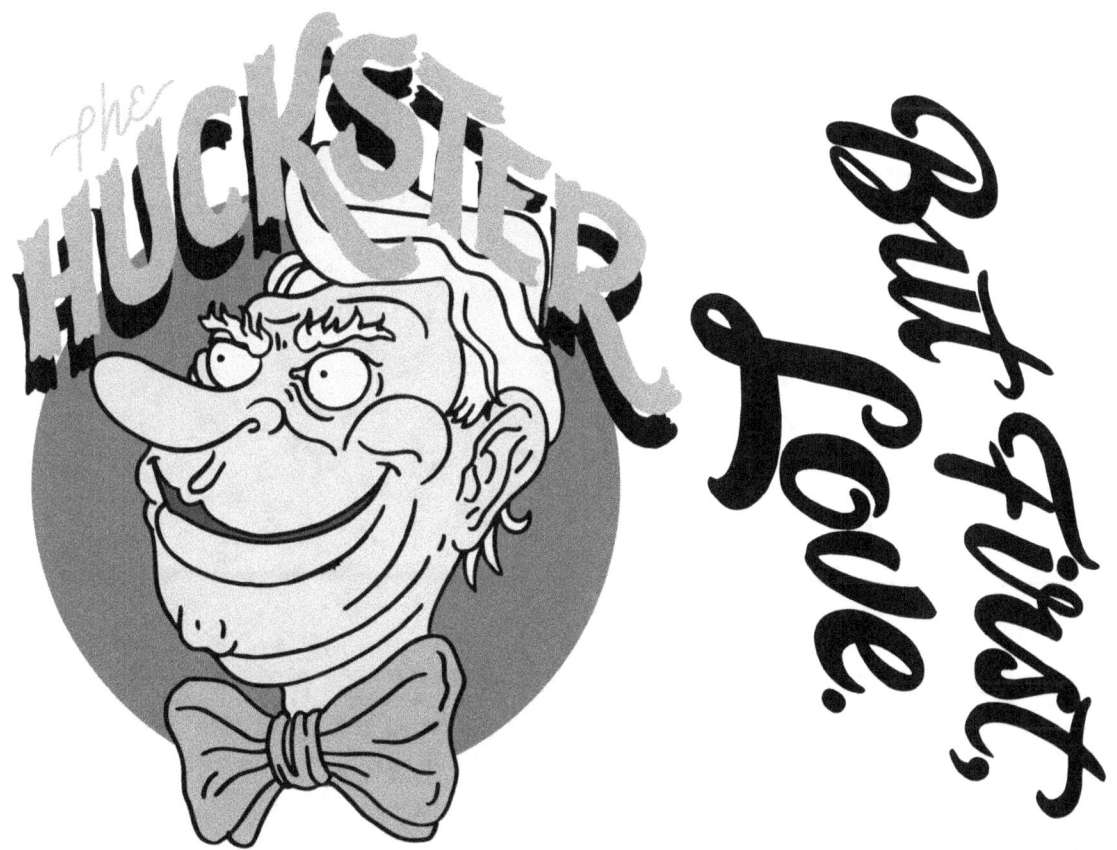

SCOUNDREL

Drifter

Stumblebum

RUFFIAN

Miscreant

Columbia TN

Mule Town TN

C.J. Hughes

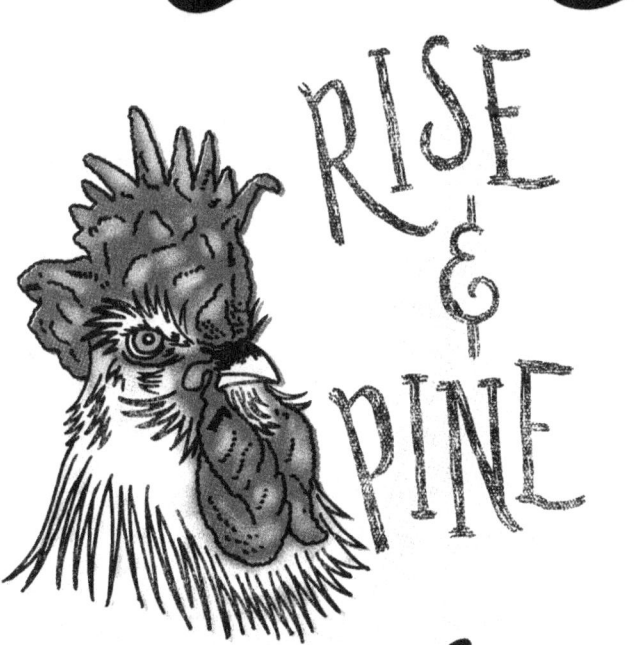

Rise & Pine

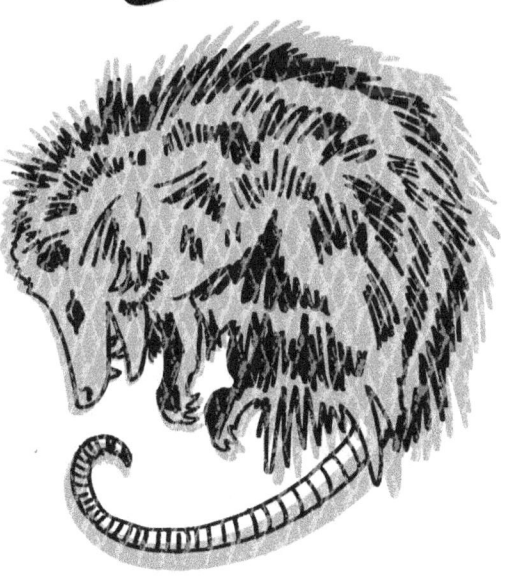

Le Michelle

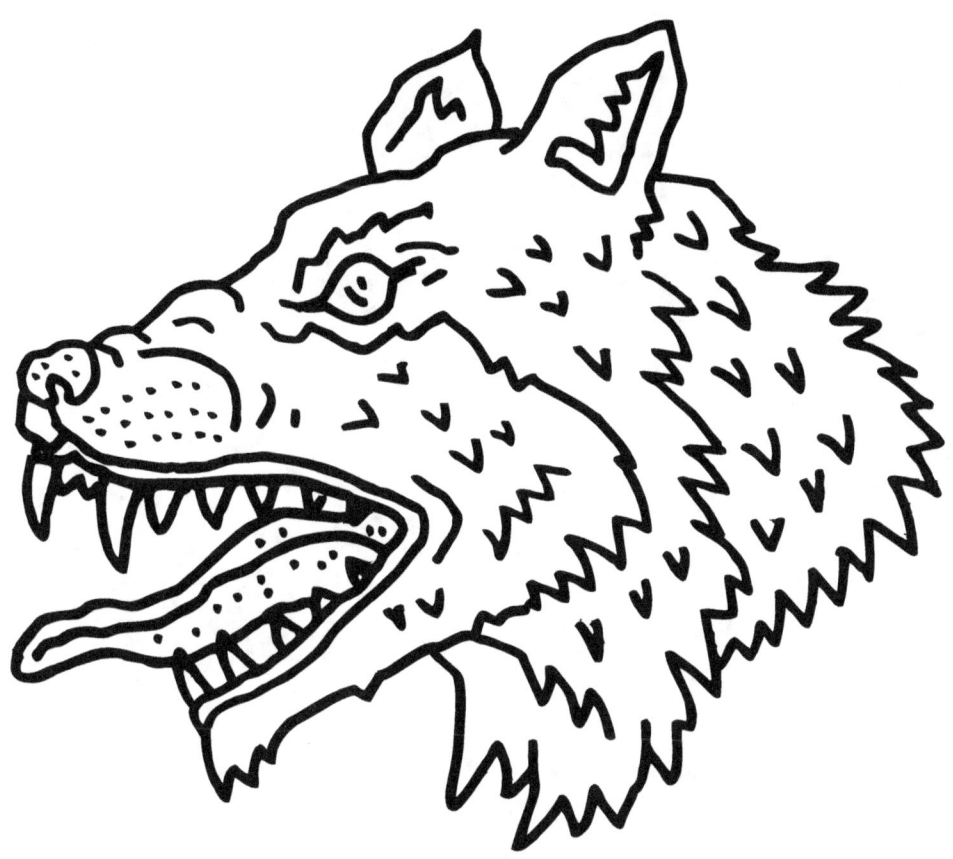

DRAWN AS AN OUTLINE CLOSING OFF ALL SHAPES. SCANNED, AUTO-TRACED TO VECTOR IN ILLUSTRATOR. SHAPES ARE BROKEN AND OUTLINE IS DISCARDED TO ACHIEVE BOTTOM DESIGN.

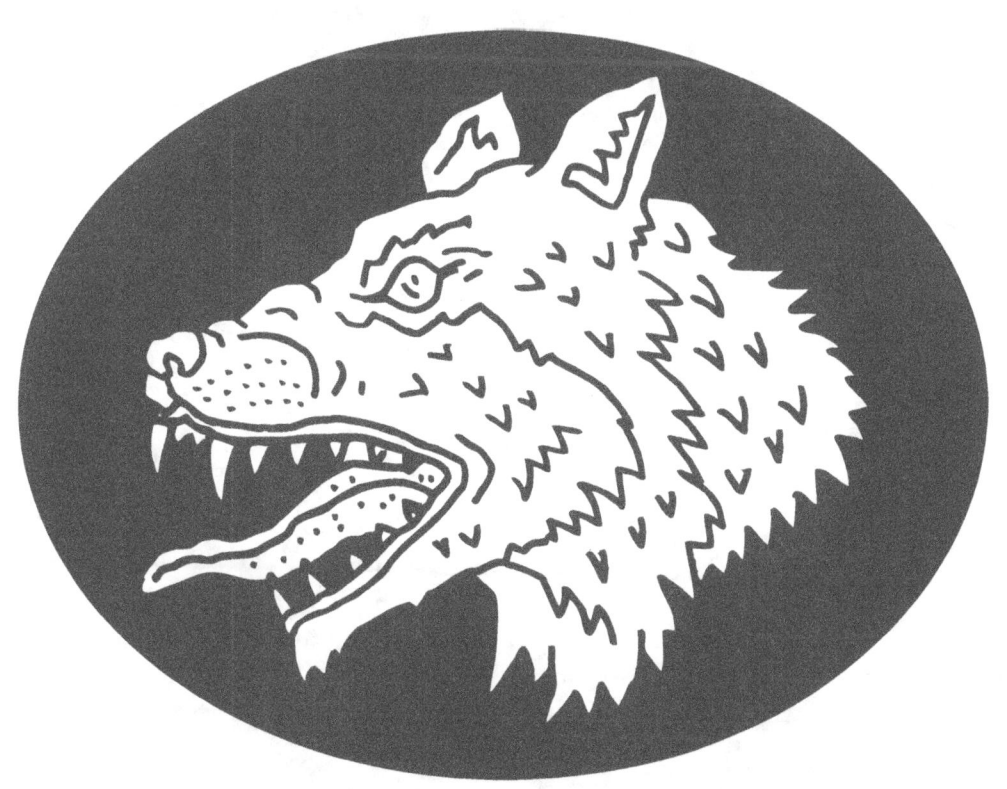

Wherever I Go BAD LUCK FOLLOWS

Tyler Childers

A B C D E F
G H I J K L
M N O P Q
R S T U V
W X Y Z

www.ingramcontent.com/pod-product-compliance
Lightning Source LLC
Chambersburg PA
CBHW080613220526
45466CB00010B/3338